W9-CBR-588

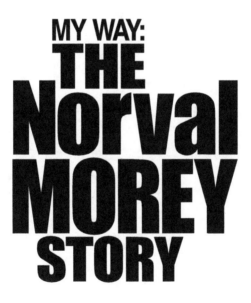

MY WAY:
THE
Norval
MOREY
STORY

By Rich Donnell
and May Lamar

THE
DONNELL
GROUP
Montgomery, Alabama

The Donnell Group
3514 Lansdowne Drive
Montgomery, AL 36111
334-303-2355
www.thedonnellgroup.com
richdonnell1955@gmail.com

Printing: Wells Printing, Montgomery, Alabama

Library of Congress Control Number: 2012921070
ISBN 978-0-9884165-1-2

First Edition

10 9 8 7 6 5 4 3 2 1

To the people of Isabella County,
back when and now.

ACKNOWLEDGMENTS

The authors wish to thank Lon Morey, CEO of Morbark Industries, for pursuing this biography of his father, Norval Morey. And right beside Lon all the way was Larry Burkholder, who celebrated 50 years with the company in 2012 and is a walking history book of Norval and Morbark.

The highlight of this project, other than completing the book, was a visit to Winn, Michigan, hometown of Norval and Morbark. And the best part of that visit was when Lon was driving Larry and myself around the rural landscape and I asked if we could visit the site where Norval had grown up. Lon and many others were under the assumption that any remains of the actual wooden home where Norval was born to Loyal and Hazel Morey were long gone. But Lon felt he could put us pretty close to where it had been, near what is now a Morbark machinery demonstration site in the woods.

We drove to the area and Lon pointed to about where he thought the house probably was. I said let's get a photo, and I took one of Lon standing beside a Morbark sign adjacent the woods. We then drove slowly out of the area, turned onto another back road and suddenly Lon halted the car. "Wait a minute!" he announced. "I think it's here!" He scampered out of the car and disappeared into the forest. Larry and I glanced at each other and knew from the sound of Lon's voice he was on to something, so we didn't wait a minute but hurried out of the car and followed Lon into the bush.

"This is it!" Lon said, as we came upon him standing beside the foundation remnants of the small log house where Norval was born and raised along with seven other siblings. Still visible were the old steps leading into what was the cellar. This was quite a remarkable discovery hidden deep in the woods.

During the course of this project we discovered many other things about Norval "Nub" Morey, thanks to the memories of his family members and acquaintances, too many to list by name here, except perhaps for one special mention.

My co-author, May Lamar, is especially grateful to have been able to meet and speak with Norval's last surviving sibling, Mrs. Lucille Morey Towne. Mrs. Towne was gracious to allow an interview, and very knowledgeable about life "back in the day."

We also wish to express our appreciation to DK Knight of Hatton-Brown Publishers, Inc., for getting this project jump-started by conducting the first round of interviews with several of Norval's family members and relatives, as well as many of Norval's most trusted employees of long ago at Morbark. DK's thorough work—supported by his own encylopedic knowledge of the timber industry during the past five decades—stood on its own, and allowed us to not have to re-interview many of those he had already interviewed, or re-research many of the developments at Morbark that he had already painstakingly documented.

I only met Norval Morey twice as I worked as an editor of several trade magazines in the wood products industry. Both times were fleeting moments; simple handshakes and a hello in the middle of crowded machinery expositions. But I would continue to hear bits and pieces about Norval Morey, and always knew there was something special about the man. We're confident that this book, the story of his life, leaves no doubt as to that.

—Rich Donnell
December 2012

CONTENTS

*Norval Morey and his siblings: sisters Lucille, left, and Mildred, with
Harry standing between them, and left to right, Milford, Ralph, Norval,
Leo and Burnell.*

ONE

Morey Farm
Winn, Michigan
Spring, 1931

It is a year and a half after the stock market crash of 1929 and 11-year-old Norval Morey is ditching school again to work on the farm. His sturdy, uncomplaining mother can sure use the help, but as Norval heats more water and minds his little brothers, he knows the main reason for his labor is so he can escape the boredom and frustration of school. There, sometimes to his embarrassment, he has trouble making sense of printed words. Norval attended less than half of 5th grade and he's managed so far to avoid a majority of the 6th. Through all of these absences, he has learned, however, to appreciate that the harder he works here at home, the happier he is in general. In a sense the farm, and all of the complexities associated with running it, are for Norval the perfect school.

No one has historically labeled the current economic collapse and steep drop in crop prices a "Great Depression" yet, but President Herbert Hoover's recent speeches over a neighboring cousin's radio reveal that even his relentless optimism has run its course and that the dead-end economy is a problem he, as president, cannot fix. The Morey family doesn't own a radio, but their neighbors the Giffords own a head set model and so does great aunt Nettie and Uncle Dave, who also live about a mile down the road. Norval and his *brothers are known to show up at either location in time for Amos and Andy or the news*

On this particular day, a Monday, Norval and his mother, Hazel Riggle Morey, are scrubbing a week's worth of family clothes on a washboard sunk in a great cast iron pot outside the four-room log house where the Morey family lives. Norval's grandfather, Loren Morey, is a skilled carpenter with a reputation for building solid barns. He had helped his son, Norval's father, Loyal, build this small log house and a small barn nearby.

Norval's father and mother sleep downstairs. Norval and his five brothers share one of the two rooms upstairs. His two sisters occupy the other. In winter, the pot bellied stove is fired up until it is red hot and what warmth it can send through the stack is enough to provide some comfort in these upper rooms. Snow sifts in around the south window and through various cracks between the logs. The family bathroom is out back. It's a one-holer. There are no shortcuts to survival at this place south of the unincorporated village of Winn in the heart of Michigan's emerging breadbasket below the Great Lakes.

Norval's father purchased the 80-acre parcel in 1915 and then went about the painstaking work of clearing the land. Eventually, with the help of family members, including eldest son Leo, he has by now cleared and stumped some 20 acres of what is considered middle of the road farmland by Isabella County standards. He devotes the majority of the acreage to growing potatoes, which he stores in and sells out of a cellar adjacent the cabin during the winter. This comprises the major portion of the family income.

Here on the farm, a long day's work doesn't ever seem to end with the sunlight, especially for Hazel. She is known to have a tender heart and a quick laugh. The tasks related to raising children and running a household seem to culminate and multiply even at the end of an already long day. Dinner chores alone, for the family of 10, take the lion's share of her evenings, even with the older children helping. Mending and sewing take another hour or so.

The pile of dirty clothes is nearly as high as Norval. It will take most of the day to scrub, wring and hang them and by that time, more than a couple of knuckles will be raw. The clothes will be done just in time for supper preparation to commence. Wood will have to be fetched along with more water from the well. The Moreys keep chickens in a coop, two cows and two plow horses in the little barn. To help make ends meet, eldest son Leo drives the egg wagon for Adams General Store in Winn. He trades store goods, such as flour, sugar and thread, for the eggs he collects from farm wives.

Small game is abundant here along the seeps and in the bogs, brush and those woods left uncut by lumbermen a generation before. Norval and his older brothers go after it with homemade traps and slingshots. Shotgun shells are a luxury rarely afforded. Norval especially loves to hunt for rabbits. By now, there are few deer left. Hunters must go north to the Upper Peninsula to find them.

Monday always is laundry day. Wednesday, Norval will cut school and he and his mother will bake a week's supply of bread together with no recipe other than the one she carries in her head. Later in the week, Norval will ditch school again to turn the soil over in the garden plot. With spring coming on fast, Norval has big plans for the family's summer and fall vegetables. He has sketched the garden in pencil on the back of an old county tax notice. Norval and Hazel will plant flowers alongside the edibles to attract pollinators and also because they love how the bright blooms dress up the place. In Norval's neat blueprint, beans and corn will go here, sunflowers here, tomatoes, cucumbers and squash here. Everything is perfectly arranged in a logical, simple pattern. After the last freeze, sometime around Memorial Day, they will get started with the planting. Norval finds success and satisfaction in the garden. Also, all the weeding, watering and thinning will mean more blessed freedom from the critical gaze of his sometime teacher, Senna Smith, and the drudgery of the one room schoolhouse known as Demlow School. There, Norval finds nothing worth sticking around for, and certainly nothing worth walking more than a mile to get to. His older siblings continue to make the trek daily. Not long ago, one or more of them might have gotten an occasional ride in their father's Model T, which Loyal had purchased in 1925. Last year, the car had to be traded for farm supplies. For now, family members catch rides when they can and otherwise travel by wagon or horseback, and when those means of transport are unavailable they travel on foot.

Later on this Monday night, with the laundry heavy on the lines out-side and the dishes finally done and Hazel is finished with her sewing, she sits down at the one luxury item on the premises, an old pump organ gleaned from her father's now boarded-up hotel and saloon in town. She plays her favorite songs, mostly old church hymns like "The Old Rugged Cross" and the children sing along in the lamplight. She finishes the concert with "I've Come to the End of a Perfect Day" and proceeds to read aloud a couple of short stories she fancies before bed. Hazel has been brought up a reader and is determined to pass the trait along to her children in spite of demands on them all that minimize the leisure that must be found for pleasure reading. Norval likes to listen to the stories. He likes the heroes. Even though he can struggle through the pages eventually, listening to his mother's voice is much easier than going through the tedious process of fingering through the words. So many skills have come so effortlessly to the boy. But as hard as he has tried, he cannot catch on to reading. The letters seem to switch around in the words.

At least one morning this week will begin with Norval feeling queasy enough to miss school. Norval's absences are mounting this school year. His parents don't force the issue because their son is a tangible asset on the farm. At least one aspect of his education seems to have taken hold, though: mathematics. Norval is a whiz with numbers.

The evening before this one, Loyal had shuffled up the cards and invited the family to a good game of Euchre. The Morey family didn't refrain just because it was Sunday, and in fact, didn't make it to church much anyway. Loyal loves the arithmetic of cards and so does his middle child, Norval. On slow days, Loyal can sometimes be found around a table in Winn, playing for pennies with his friends. The Morey kids will play cards and sing the old hymns together for the rest of their lives.

Norval "Nub" Morey was born on December 29, 1919, the fourth Morey child, following Leo (1914), Burnell (1916) and Mildred (1918). By the time of the Great Depression, Ralph (1922), Lucille (1924), Milford (1926) and Harry (1928) had joined the family. Years later in a taped interview, Norval said, "By 1930 there were eight

Hazel and Loyal Morey with their children.

of us kids, plus my mother and father. We were living in a little log house, which, by today's standards, would be pretty crowded.

"The times I remember most growing up were in the Depression years. Everyone talked about how hard up they were but I didn't realize we were hard up. We never went without food. We didn't have any money or new clothes, things like that, but as long as everyone was in the same boat, it didn't seem to make much difference."

Before Norval needed to shave, he knew how to bake, garden, cut timber, hunt, trap and perform any chore on the farm. He made his own toys. All of the Morey kids did. "We played games outside in winter and summer both," Norval said. "We could pretty much do as we pleased after the chores were done." In addition to laundry and baking, those chores for Norval included the summer canning of peas, corn, peaches and beans, cutting wood, tending to his younger brothers and regular butchering of chickens, rabbits, turkeys, hogs and squirrels for meat.

Norval's youthful propensity for cooking never left him. His daughter Betty Morey Robison recalled, "My father was a natural cook. He never used a recipe. He would bake enormous batches of bread and it was wonderful. He would bake a cake the same way and it beat anything I could do. He learned how from helping my grandmother."

Marge Gifford Barrett, who grew up less than a mile from the Morey farm and walked past their place on her way to school every morning, remembered the intoxicating aroma of baking bread.

"My sister and I would walk by and smell that bread baking and think it was the most wonderful smell on Earth," Barrett said. "Sometimes Hazel would invite us in to have some."

As a girl, Marge Barrett—whose mother, Susie, was Hazel Morey's life-long best friend—occasionally spent the night in the Morey cabin with Norval's sister, Lucille. "One night it was snowing hard and coming through the cracks between the logs," she said.

Every month of the year, the two families and others gathered for a potluck dinner. Marge recalled one particular potluck night, which fell on the day after a ravaging hail storm had come through Winn and destroyed everyone's crops.

"Everyone was so quiet, and that was unusual for this group," she said. "I decided that night that I was not going to marry a farmer."

What is now Isabella County, in the very center of the Lower Michigan mitt, was once vast woodland known as "Ojibiway Besse" or place of the Chippewa. Over a span of 10,000 years, various clans of the Chippewa, including the Beaver and Saginaw, used the area as a winter hunting ground. Father Henry Nouvel spent the winter of 1675 in the area but it was more than 150 years later when Isabella County was set off as a county.

Known for having the greatest white pine and hardwood forests in the Great Lakes Region, the area was a natural lightning rod for the logging industry once settlement of the America west began in earnest. By the mid 1800s logging camps and sawmills were popping up all over the region, changing the ancient landscape and pushing out the native Chippewa tribes.

In 1855, the first of two treaties establishing a 130,000-acre reservation in what would become Isabella County was signed between the tribes and the U.S. Government. (Regardless of a shaky beginning to the reserved land due to some reported swindling by early timber barons, the tribe today operates one of the largest casinos in the Midwest on nearly 200 square miles of tribal land in the county.)

In 1859, the Michigan legislature officially established Isabella County, naming it after the Spanish queen who helped finance the 1492 voyage of Christopher Columbus. Over the next decade, townships were formed, the names of many of which reflect the sentiments of their founders. Fremont Township, where Winn is located, was organized in 1863 and is named for Union General John C. Fremont. Sherman Township is named for Union General William Tecumseh Sherman. Union Township, Lincoln Township and Gilmore Township (which is named for Union General Quincy Adam Gillmore but misspelled) all are products of Civil War times.

Farmers came on the heels of the loggers to this area of slow rolling hills, sandy as well as loamy soils and tributaries of the Pine River winding their way through the expansive countryside.

According to local historian Wayne Barrett, the village now known as Winn began as a wooden box nailed to a tree for dissemination of the U.S. Mail. The community's first postmaster, Frank Williams, a native of Wynn, England, supposedly chose the name "Winn" to honor his hometown. In 1867, a log house replaced the old box. As late as 1872, Winn merely was the name of a post office in the midst of dozens of farms and lumber camps. There were no established towns or businesses in the township.

All that changed in 1875, when a young man from Ohio, William Wiley Dush, purchased 40 acres of land in Section 15 with dreams of starting his own town. From early maps, the original plat looks like nothing more than a spec in the center of the 36-square-mile Fremont Township. Dush, whose last name is derived from the Hungarian nickname for "rich guy," had come to the area with his father. The pair had money to invest. According to Todd family records, Dush's mother was a double cousin of Mary Todd Lincoln and Dush and his father had been left some Todd money.

Dush sectioned off this new property, setting up a shopping district and a residential area, with the intention of serving the lumbermen and farmers that surrounded him. He also had plans to build a sawmill to produce and sell lumber for the anticipated growth that would be certain to follow this endeavor.

Dush called the new town "Dushville." Introduction of a new name to the area did not sit well with some, but the fallout would not occur for several years.

The prevailing hope was that Dushville would eventually get a railroad and the excitement this caused spurred building and development over the next several years. A Grand Army of the Republic Hall was built. A newspaper, *The Dushville Banner*, was established by the local lyceum, along with a baseball team, a barbershop, a bank, three general stores, a drugstore, a bowling alley and a large hotel. Dushville brought in two doctors and an undertaker.

While it is not clear whether they owned it or simply managed it, Ed and Eliza Riggle ran the new Commercial House Hotel, Saloon and Dance Hall. Each had moved to Isabella County from Warren, Ohio— Ed to join other family members who had proceeded him. Their daughter, Norval's mother, Hazel, was born at the Commercial House in 1892. She is listed in the U.S. Census of 1900 as a 7-year-old living with her parents at the hotel.

With the success of his town, W.W. Dush began to branch out. He opened his own general store in addition to the sawmill. Businessman John Starkweather also opened a sawmill in competition with Dush. Starkweather later opened a general store across the street from Dush, which was outside the entrepreneur's original town plat. Starkweather refused to acknowledge that his store was part of Dushville. Instead, he took to calling his side of the street "Hardscrabble" in defiance of the wishes of his chief competitor. Others outside Dush's domain still referred to themselves as residents of Winn. Things got even more confusing when, after having been named postmaster in 1882, Dush managed to have the official name of the post office changed from Winn to Dushville. Add to that various lumber camps with their own individual names scattered about the township and the mix-ups and missed connections continued to mount.

Then, on New Year's Eve, 1888, Dush's steam-powered sawmill over in Broomfield Township exploded while Dush and the fireman, John Carr, were tinkering with the water level of the engine. The *Banner* carried the story of the tragedy:

"Our informant says that every bone in Dush's body was crushed so that it was perfectly limp. Carr's body was cut completely in two and the two portions thrown in opposite directions."

Dush, 44, left a wife and two children behind. The Broomfield mill was the third and last to detonate under the enterprising Ohio native's watch.

Dushville never got its railroad spur. Local loggers and sawmills had to continue hauling their lumber and timber to market by wagon. After a petition was circulated, the Michigan State Legislature changed the official name of the post office back to Winn in 1895.

Eventually, as the big lumber camps and sawmills moved on farther west, more farmers from the Ohio Valley and points east, along with immigrants from Europe, continued to move in to Isabella County. They came in to buy the "timbered out" parcels and wrestle the stumps left behind. In the lower part of the state, throughout Newaygo County, lay the vast mixed grass range called the Big Prairie. Settlers there built on the edges of the prairie, which was ringed with white pine forests, so they could log the forests and cultivate the grasslands. Eventually, because farming displaced the topsoil, the name of the range was changed to the Big Prairie Desert. This area would later produce Michigan's own version of the Dust Bowl.

In the mid 1890s, Israel Moray (His name is spelled "Morey" on several U.S. Census reports and "Moray" on his tombstone), his sons, George and Loren, and their wives and children arrived from Williams County, Ohio looking for opportunity and a place to grow potatoes, as they had back home. They chose Fremont Township, well north of the one great prairie in Michigan.

While Israel had brought his family to Winn from Ohio, he had started out married life in Huron, New York. This was along the shores of Lake Ontario and the Great Sodus Bay. Just before the Civil War, in 1860, Israel listed his occupation on the U.S. Census as "day labor" and reported that he came to the U.S. from Canada in 1850. His wife, Mary Ann Conklin, was from the Seneca Falls area. Wayne County, New York had excused Israel from the Civil War draft due to his Canadian birth.

The future looked bright for farming. Ellis Island recently had opened in New York Harbor as a receiving station to process an endless stream of immigrants coming from Europe. The resulting population explosion in America would mean more mouths to feed. The rich, former woodlands of Fremont Township were plentiful and cheap, pocked as they were with old growth stumps. Israel's oldest son, Loren's older brother, John, had stayed behind in Ohio to teach school.

In 1894, Loren's wife, Emma Jane, gave birth to the couple's second son, Loyal. He was the first in a long line of Morey children to be born over the coming years in Fremont Township.

For the first several years in Winn, the Morey men worked day labor jobs to save money and learn the lay of the land. Loren earned a good reputation as a builder and earned decent wages erecting barns across the county, some of them still standing.

In 1899, the Moreys put their money into three 40-acre tracts of land just south of the newly renamed town of Winn. Israel and Loren's land adjoined. George's acreage was less than a mile away. Loren's married sister, Nettie Moray Riggle, and her husband settled within a mile of Israel and Loren's farmland. The Morey family went to farming potatoes, and multiplying.

The name "Morey" is an ancient one with its roots in France, Scotland and Ireland. As immigrants had their names translated from Gaelic versions into English, fluctuations were abundant. Today, there are any number of spelling variations, including Moray, Moret, Morrey, Murray, Mowry and Moore. While Norval Morey's grandfather, Israel, often had spelled it "Moray," genealogical researchers of the family line tend to agree that Israel is most likely descended from John Morey of Augusta, Ontario in Canada.

If that is true, Norval Morey was descended from a line of Morey men dating back to the original 13 Colonies starting with the appearance of George Morey in Bristol, Rhode Island in the mid 1600's. George's son, John, born in Bristol in 1684, was a private in the First Massachusetts Regiment during the French Indian War. John's son, Ephraim, born in 1710, was an old man during the Revolutionary War but lived long enough to participate in the very first U.S. Census count in 1790. In it, he and his wife, Abigail, parents of 16 children, are listed as living in Charlton City, Massachusetts. Ephraim's son, Simeon, was just the right age to fight in the Revolution and did so. Simeon's son, Samuel, who is reputed to have been loyal to the British, moved to Augusta, Canada in 1784. This is where John Morey was born in 1800 and in 1835, is where Israel Moray might have been born, although no direct evidence links Israel to John or the small village of Augusta in Grenville and Leeds County, Ontario. In U.S. Census data, Israel reports he and his father were both born in Canada East. At the time, churches were the main repositories for birth, death and marriage records in this part of Canada. Today, many such records, if they were kept at all, are lost.

The migration of this line of the Morey family roughly mirrors the westward course of the Erie Canal, a common migration pattern of the region.

Why Norval Morey's grandfather, Israel, did not go along with the historical spelling of the name is a question that remains unanswered. While "Israel Moray" is the name etched in granite in Winn's Union Cemetery, and his son John Moray's headstone also bears the spelling of "Moray," it is "Morey" that is carved on the nearby grave of his other son, Loren. Loren was Norval's grandfather and this is the spelling that stuck with Norval. Other family members, including Norval's brother, Burnell, seemed to have fluctuated back and forth between Morey and Moray during their lives, but were buried as Morey. To date, there are but four Morays (Israel and his wife and John and his wife) and 24

Moreys buried in Fremont Township's Union Cemetery. All are from the same extended family.

Whatever else happened in Winn after its emergence from the egocentric name change and during the years Loyal was growing up on his family's nearby potato farm, this much is certain: Winn reached its peak. After 1910, the population began steadily to decline. Unlike San Francisco, which was all but destroyed by the earthquake of 1906, very few townspeople stuck around Winn to build it back up after the railroad didn't come and logging moved west. With the people went three general stores, the hat shop, the doctor's office, the newspaper, the baseball team and the bowling balls. Around this same time, the newspaper folded.

When the Commercial House Hotel, Saloon and Dance Hall went in the red, Norval's grandfather, Ed Riggle, bought a plow and took up farming again.

Israel Moray and his sons continued working their land regardless of the changes in town and by all accounts, prospered.

In October of 1913, 19-year-old store clerk Loyal Morey and 21-year-old Hazel Riggle from the hotel were married. The newlyweds were distant cousins, as Loyal's Aunt Nettie had married Hazel's cousin, David Riggle.

In 1915, Israel Moray died at age 80. Around the time of Israel's death in Winn, his newlywed grandson Loyal came up with the money to put down on 80 acres of mostly un-cleared woods and brush lands just south of Winn. It was not too far from his parents' place.

Loyal Morey had been granted exemption from service in World War I citing his responsibility for a wife and children. Hazel named their fourth child "Norval" for the soldier who had accompanied her brother Harry's body home from that same war. This was eventually shortened to "Nub" by younger siblings mispronouncing it or older ones making comparisons between Norval and his taller cousin, "Bub." Whatever the genesis, it stuck. Norval's nickname was so longstanding, his sister cannot remember how it got started. And while Lucille Morey Towne is not sure what the nickname implies, she does know it was her brother's name as long as she knew him.

The young Morey family was adept at entertaining themselves. Playing cards was a favorite pastime, along with hunting, swimming and socializing with the children of neighbors. Norval said later and on more than one occasion that once the chores were done, the Morey kids were free to go.

"We occasionally played spin the bottle with the Morey boys," said neighbor Marge Gifford Barrett. "They were a crew, I tell you. Ralph (Norval's younger brother) pulled a snake out of his pocket and threw it at me one day on my way to school, and that's when I formed my opinion of him. Harry and Milford were the babies and they were full of mischief. They would go off hunting and stay gone for three days while Hazel worried herself sick about them."

Many years later, Marge would marry Thurman Barrett, the brother of Norval's first wife, Phyllis. Thurman, a carpenter by trade, and Norval partnered early on and remained friends and colleagues throughout their lives.

Marge says Norval Morey always was someone you could count on.

"Once, when my father came down with flu, I was put in charge of the milking. Then, I came down with it, too," she said. "Norval came over and he did the milking until we got well. That was the kind of friend he was."

While the Morey family couldn't afford the luxury of a radio when Norval was a child, they never went hungry. One reason is that from the time they were able, they all worked for their meals. Whether it was hunting, hoeing, canning, milking or swapping eggs for sugar, food procurement was a constant challenge for the children and their mother. Loyal Morey, meanwhile, did all in his power to earn the cash needed to pay the farm's mortgage and property taxes. He sold firewood to supplement the income from potatoes.

"We grew lots and lots of potatoes," Lucille recalled. "My brothers dug them with forks and we picked them up. Dad had a cave-like place that he stored them in and throughout the winter they would come and get them with trucks."

At 16, Lucille left the family and went out on her own. She found employment as a babysitter in nearby Mount Pleasant and later worked as a maid. In the year 2012, at age 87, her gentle demeanor and quick laugh gave a glimpse of what her mother, Hazel, might have been like.

"When we were growing up my sister, Mildred, was known as the religious one," Towne said. "I was known as the drinking one, but that all changed in 1985 when I accepted the Lord."

By today's standards, the kids in the Morey family joined the "real world" at young ages. Nearly all were out of the house and supporting themselves by 16. All was not hard work and drudgery, however. Perhaps Norval's older brothers were aware of the biggest sports story to ever hit the region. Sometime around 1922, in neighboring Wise Township, Frederick Methner's 12 sons played the Detroit Tigers in a best of three series. The Methner sons took two games of the three and won the admiration of every baseball fan in the area. Up until this storied sporting feat, the explosion at Dush's sawmill was the most extraordinary thing to have happened in the vicinity.

And while the work never stopped, it did slow down enough at times for the Morey kids to round up their neighbor friends and spend summer afternoons swimming at a place called Five Springs. "It had those bubbly waters coming up out of the ground," Lucille said. "We spent a lot of time there and climbing trees, too."

The most drastic effects of the Great Depression reached Isabella County just as Norval was turning 12.

"My father and mother worked very hard," Norval Morey said. "They had almost no money at all after paying the taxes and the interest on the farm. I don't ever remember either one of them buying any new clothes when I was growing up."

"Black Thursday," as it was called and the ensuing economic quagmire darkened the once-vibrant economy in Michigan. In Detroit, auto production, which had reached an all-time high in 1929 of more than five million vehicles, plunged to two million in 1930. By 1933, production was down an astonishing 75 percent from the pre-Depression peak. The oil discovery and subsequent rush that in 1928 had quickly made nearby Mount Pleasant the oil capital of Michigan skidded to a halt.

The market crash also led to the closure of nearly every coal mine in the Upper Peninsula. A couple of years after the collapse, half of all non-farm workers in the state would be without jobs.

As it turned out, however, the Great Depression was good to young Norval in at least one way. It was his ticket out of the seventh grade. Farmers like the Moreys had jobs, but farm prices had taken the plunge along with everything else. Making the mortgage payment was getting harder and harder. Loyal turned to his older son, Leo, for help with a small firewood operation. When Leo got admitted into the newly formed Civilian Conservation Corps and moved away, Loyal found himself without someone to haul the wood into town. Norval quickly volunteered for wood chopping and delivering duty and forever shucked the dreaded one-room Demlow School from his life.

"I started the seventh grade and I think I went two or three days," he recalled years later. "I got excused to haul wood and never went back." Throughout his life Norval would joke that his teacher told him

Norval is in the first row, sixth from left. He was already known as Nub in this 1930 photo, and was 11 years old. His days at Demlow School were numbered. His brother, Ralph, is first row fourth from left; sister Lucille is second row far right; brother Burnell is third row standing second from left; and sister Mildred is third row seventh from left.

he was smarter than her and didn't need to come back to school, which is why he quit.

"There were usually 22 kids in the school up to 30," Norval said. "The teacher would have to teach grades from beginners up to the eighth grade. So it was very difficult for one teacher to be able to pay a lot of attention to any one kid, especially if they were a little slow in reading and spelling. They usually got behind."

Norval was now free from the obligation of going to school, but his freedom came at a cost. He was now a working man, and as such shouldered a heavy set of responsibilities around the farm. As he had all along, though, young Norval found the hard work far superior than formal education.

In the darkest days of the economic calamity everything was on the line for the Morey clan and nearly all of their neighbors and kin.

"It was right in the Depression and the way my father kept from losing the farm and everything else was to cut wood one winter and deliver it the next winter to customers in the little town. That helped pay the taxes and bought what groceries we had," Norval said.

"We hauled the wood on a wagon that would hold two cords. He would load it up in the morning and I would haul it to Winn and throw it off and come back. At lunchtime, we would go load up another load and I would haul it and be back by five or six o'clock at night. Usually, I would haul two loads one day and the following day I would haul one load. We cut and delivered this wood to the customers for $1.25 a cord. Some days I would have to deliver it and pile it up for the customer the way they wanted it. It was tough work but I would still rather do that than have to go to school. It was quite obvious that going to school wasn't going to educate me any further."

Norval was the only one of his siblings not to at least finish the 8th grade.

Over the next two years, teenaged Norval became both his mother and his father's right hand man. In addition now to baking, keeping the garden and washing clothes, Norval learned to drive the horses, plow and drag, pull and clear stumps and fix whatever got broken. He

All about potatoes. Norval is riding at left, with Milford, Loyal and Ralph

excelled at this work and when he was done with the chores at the Morey farm, Norval would hire himself out to other farm families.

"I could do almost any job that a hired man could have done," he said. "My father would praise me to other men and tell them what a good man I was on the farm and that kept me blown up to where he didn't have any problem getting me to work."

Norval never expected any pay for working at home, but sometimes on a Saturday night his dad gave him 50 cents or a dollar. When he contracted out his skills to the neighbors, he usually received 75 cents to a dollar a day.

Norval liked to stay in motion, a personality trait that he carried for the rest of his life. His daughter recalled that years later, when her dad was at the helm of a major manufacturing company, she would see him out hoeing and weeding his flowers at sunrise before heading to work at Morbark Industries. For as long as he lived he planted long, vibrant rows of summer impatiens, all along the front of his house and behind it as well. He planted so many each summer that his rambling home on Lake Isabella gained some notoriety as a tourist destination. People would drive up from other parts of the county just to see Norval's annual handiwork. Long-time associate Larry Burkholder recalled those days.

"When the nursery man saw Norval coming every spring, he would be mighty happy," Burkholder said.

Norval's sister, Lucille, recalled her teenage brother as "always happy and always working at something. He would go down and help Aunt Nettie and Uncle Dave who lived about a half mile from us. Aunt Nettie was a sister to my grandpa Morey. They had a nice house and they had a radio and things we didn't have. Norval became close friends with their son, Guy. I never heard Norval say an angry word. Some of my brothers could be kind of mean but he never was. He was always good to me. He was a giving person."

Norval and his brother, Burnell, who was three years older, were in business together from their earliest years and even during this time of scarce wages became successful at turning a profit through innovative thinking.

"At a very early age, my brother, Burnell, and I tried to figure out ways of making money. We did everything from berry picking to bounty hunting," Norval said.

At that time in Isabella County, the government paid a two-cents-per-head bounty on sparrows, a quarter-per-head bounty on crows and a dime for a set of rat's ears.

"We would take flashlights at night in barns and shake ropes and get the sparrows flying," Norval recalled. "They would fly toward the flashlight and we would catch them. Here's the way we got crows: We didn't have money enough to buy shotgun shells, so we would hunt crows' nests. As soon as the feathers got on the young crows we could climb up and shake them out and get 25 cents each."

Norval got into the habit of saving part of his earnings. Money-making became like a favorite game.

"Rats were everywhere. You could trap them and the county paid a dime for their ears. We had a buddy in Montcalm County where they paid a dime apiece for their tails. So, we'd swap our tails for his ears and make 20 cents off one rat."

Norval and Burnell began earning enough to buy their own clothes, save and still have some spending money.

1933 was the deepest trough of the Depression. Massive dust storms were becoming a serious problem in the Great Plains states, with the largest, most famous one yet to come. Michigan would, in May of 1934, be directly in the path of one dust cloud 1,500 miles long, 900 miles across and two miles high that was said to have started in Wyoming and Montana and picked up dirt along the way. Before dissipating over the Atlantic, the dust covered over one third of the country.

With winter coming on that year, work on the Morey farm was beginning to slow down. Norval was anxious to take a break and had managed to save up around $5. When a couple of his buddies suggested they go north and try deer hunting, Norval jumped at the chance.

"Back in the 30's there were no deer in this area," Norval recalled. "If you wanted to hunt deer, you had to go farther north around Houghton Lake and farther. I was about to be 15 and Stanley Courser and Iry Dailey and me decided we'd go up north deer hunting. Stanley had an uncle up in Glennie and he knew if we got up there we could stay in his barn during the hunting season. So we put all our money together and had about 15 bucks and headed up north."

When the boys got to Houghton Lake, Stanley's uncle informed them of a cabin for rent on the lake that he thought they could afford. The boys rented a small but furnished cabin and settled in for two weeks of hunting deer. The experience of letting loose from daily chores and family obligations was great adventure. When deer season was over, Norval and his pals decided they should look for a job and stay put for the winter.

"We thought we could get a job cutting cedar fence posts or wood or some kind of a job in the woods, which was about all any of us knew how to do in the winter," Norval recalled.

After a few days, the boys ran into a man named Fields who was having a hard time getting his six employees to show up for work cutting saw logs and fence posts. When the crew did show up, their work was shoddy. Norval suggested that he and his friends could outwork

Fields' men and Fields agreed to give them a try. He left the trio from Winn in the woods with a tract to cut and went to Detroit, telling them he'd decide whether or not to hire them permanently based on what he found when he got back.

"So Stanley went to cutting fence posts and Iry and I cut logs," Norval said. "To impress the old boy, Iry and I worked like hell while he was gone and laid down a lot of logs and cut them up. In three days, we cut more than the other six guys had done in probably two weeks."

When Fields returned he took a look at what the boys had produced while he was gone and immediately offered them cutting work for the rest of the winter.

"We said we would but we'd like to have a little more money than what he was paying," Norval said. "I think he was paying us two dollars a day. He agreed as long as we kept up the good work. Not only that, he laid off the rest of his crew."

He also offered the boys a free shanty to stay in. It was 8x10 and had a sawdust floor, but it had a bunk and a stove, and was closer to their work. The boys gave up their rented cabin and moved in for the remainder of the winter.

Just before Christmas, Fields informed the boys he had temporarily sidetracked into the Christmas tree business. So the three friends spent a couple of weeks cutting, dragging out and loading the small trees on trucks bound for the shopping districts of Detroit. Stanley went back home soon after, but Iry and Norval stayed on with Fields in northern Michigan and cut logs until spring.

"I believe he wound up paying us three dollars and a half a day, which in them days was pretty good wages," Norval said. "I saved quite a little money."

Norval returned to the family farm in Winn in the spring of 1935 to assist his dad and worked there through the summer and into the fall. Then word came that electricity was headed toward Winn soon and that the Rural Electric Association was putting together crews in the area to clear the rights of way for the placement of power lines.

Now going on 16, Norval, who had been working for no wages

since returning home, applied for work with a contractor named Frank Ryman after he heard what they were paying the crew. "They paid big wages then—35 cents an hour," Norval recalled. Ryman hired him and Norval cut trees for several weeks before the foreman wanted him to start climbing trees because he didn't have any tree pruners. Norval did that job into the following spring when the REA finished up its work in the area. The contractor, Ryman, would re-surface after the war and figure prominently in the birth of Morbark.

The foreman of the crew Norval worked on then asked Norval to accompany him to a job in Ohio trimming around live power lines and removing limbs. The dangerous duty allowed Norval an increase in pay to 45 cents an hour. They worked throughout Ohio and Michigan and the money was coming in, though Norval didn't crave all of the climbing involved. He said sometimes he was so high up he couldn't see the ground through the "clouds," and sickness would overcome him as he felt like he was swaying. Norval decided not to go back to the farm that summer, where the wages were spotty. The next summer he went to work for McNeil Tree Service, a company that contracted up and down the Eastern U.S. The work took Norval down to North Carolina and other parts of the South, and then up to the Northeast and Pennsylvania. He was climbing daily now but as the weather turned cold the trees became icy and Norval grew weary of the working conditions.

Then word came from his older brother, Burnell, that there was money to be made, lots of it, in the great white pine forests of northern Idaho. A couple of years earlier, Clell Morey, who was Burnell and Norval's uncle (Loyal's brother), had enticed Burnell to come to Idaho and take up falling and bucking for Potlatch Forests Inc. in the Clearwater River Forests of the Bitterroot Range nestled into the Rocky Mountains.

Clell himself had migrated to the Lewiston, Idaho area years earlier and found work in the woods, doing every conceivable job but eventually finding his niche as a river log drive chief. The Potlatch river log drive was legendary and local residents came out to view this spectacular demonstration every April and May after the Chinook winds had reared up and the snow and ice began to melt, turning the rivers into torrential flood paths.

Trees that were felled the previous summer were skidded to a preparation site or landing, bucked into log lengths and loaded into river log flumes (not unlike the flumes seen today in water amusement parks), which carried the logs along tributaries into various points of the main North Fork of the Clearwater River coming out of the Bitterroot. A dozen flumes carried as much as 40 million board feet of logs into the river to await the spring thaw. The drive lasted up to three weeks and covered 100 miles, beginning in the upper reaches of the North Fork of the Clearwater River, moving southwest and then north and then southwest again until the North Fork merged into the Clearwater River, and then a long southwest route before reaching the confluence of the Clearwater and Snake rivers and dumping into the log ponds of the large white pine sawmill operated by Potlatch at Lewiston.

It took months of preparation, especially in the construction of the flumes and the camps. It also required courageous workers to man the drive. River men rode in 22-foot bright red bateau flat bottom boats manned by powerful oarsmen. At the end of the boat was a man with a long pike pole and a cant hook. As many as 30 men were needed for a complete log drive team. During the day they steered logs, retrieved stray logs hung up on the banks or sand bars, and broke up notorious logjams. During a logjam, more than 10 million board feet could bottleneck perhaps due to shallow water or other geographical roadblock introduced by the river. Often they left their boats and tread the giant timbers with calk boots, jumping from log to log, bobbing and weaving, using a peavey to try and dislodge the jam, all the while competing with the rushing river current. When the jam began to break and the logs began to separate and move, there was hell to pay as the men scampered over them until they found safe footing.

Accompanying the men on the river journey were large wanigans mounted on rafts. These carried along the cookhouses and bunkhouses. Here the men found dry clothing, food fit for a king and comfortable beds, and a commissary that sold them cigarettes, gloves, Copenhagen, boot nails and socks.

When Burnell joined Clell in Idaho, Clell took a year off from his river jamming job to go back into the woods as a faller and train his nephew. Burnell relayed back to Norval that he wouldn't believe the size of the pines, but that felling them wasn't any more dangerous than dodging hot wires as Norval had been doing, and the pay was unlike anything they had ever heard of. Burnell also advised his little brother to come out as soon as he could because they both were likely heading off to war pretty soon.

By the beginning of 1938, Adolf Hitler and his Nazi Party had seized power in Germany, and in a few months would enter Austria and declare it part of the German Third Reich. Later in the year Hitler's Nazis burned synagogues, destroyed Jewish shops and killed Jews at random during a night that became forever known as Kristallnacht and which revealed Hitler's intentions for "the Jewish question" as he called it. Also during the year, leaders of Great Britain and France would meet with Hitler in a desperate attempt to avoid war. They acceded to most of his territorial demands but few Europeans expected peace to prevail. Meanwhile, in Asia, Japan continued its hostile invasion of China. World War II seemed inevitable to more and more Americans.

The Depression had doomed Herbert Hoover's re-election for pres-

Burnell, at left with unidentified worker, persuaded Norval to work in the big timber out West.

ident and he lost the 1932 election to the governor of New York, Franklin D. Roosevelt. FDR's New Deal jobs program put some of the populace back to work and provided renewed spirit throughout the country. Following Roosevelt's re-election in 1936, the country's economy and production rebounded to pre-Depression levels. Unemployment remained high, though not as staggering as a few years earlier. But as Norval considered following his brother to the Northwest, the economy and industrial production took a sharp downturn that would last through most of 1938. This likely figured into Norval's thinking.

Meanwhile the other big news during this period was Amelia Earhart's plane disappearing during a flight across the Pacific Ocean; the Hindenburg bursting into flames as it attempted to moor at Lakehurst, New Jersey; and Joe Louis, the Brown Bomber, becoming world heavyweight boxing champion and then defending his crown with a first round knockout of Germany's Max Schmeling.

Norval liked the idea of seeing the West, especially when he heard how much could be made cutting virgin timber.

"Burnell was making quite a bit of money," Norval said. "He didn't have to convince me too hard to come out because I was ready to quit climbing and pruning like I was doing but I'd still be cutting which is what I knew."

Norval left his tree-pruning job in late February of 1938 and met up with his brother at Lewiston, where Burnell did his best to alert Norval to the dangers he was likely to face in the Potlatch forests. There were many, as A.M. Prouty noted in his book, *More Deadly Than War: Pacific Coast Logging, 1827-1981:*

"Logging was then, and remains today, a business where a man literally had better know how to run for his life."

While Norval was no stranger to the risks of cutting timber in the woods, this was logging on a much larger scale than what he'd seen back East.

Lewiston was a bustling city of 10,000 that offered plenty of whiskey establishments for the Morey brothers to take in while they got reacquainted. At first, the brothers didn't see much of Clell, who was back to making preparations for the upcoming river log drive. In addition to loggers and sawmillers combing the streets and all-night bars, cowboys were everywhere, too. Lewiston was a rodeo and roundup mecca. Big money competitions, auctions and herds being driven to market were regular occurrences around the town. With spring approaching, the activity was now beginning to increase. There are stories that Norval took to wearing a Stetson hat based on the time he spent among the cowboys in Idaho.

Because it was a couple of months before the woods would open up for summer falling, Norval found work as a laborer on a fruit farm to tide him over. Burnell, meanwhile, had met the love of his life in Clara Schwartz, a petite beauty who had grown up in Lewiston. Clara was a popular girl and a devoted Catholic. Burnell was smitten from the start. They would eventually have seven children together.

Norval Morey was 18 years old and eager to have his shot at the big timber. Building crates in anticipation of the summer fruit harvest likely seemed rather tame in comparison. By summer, though, Norval would become part of one of the most spectacular forest operations in the legendary history of the Northwest timber industry.

Potlatch Forests, Inc., had been formed in 1931 by the merger of Potlatch Lumber Company, Edward Rutledge Timber Company and Clearwater Timber Company. The prevailing investor in all of those operations and in the northern Idaho timberland to support them was the Weyerhaeuser family. Frederick Weyerhaeuser, who had built a formidable lumber business in the Midwest, began looking westward as timberland in the east was cut-out and as the railroad infrastructure began to take hold. His most famous timberland purchase was 900,000 acres of Washington state forest from Northern Pacific Railway. He established his first office adjacent the railway's main office in Tacoma, Washington.

This was the birth of Weyerhaeuser Company.

Frederick Weyerhaeuser also was interested in the big pine timberlands of northern Idaho. At the turn of the century, he and his partners purchased 40,000 acres, much of it on the upper reaches of the Clearwater River, and continued to purchase more in the region. His son, Charles, was the first president of Potlatch Lumber Company when it formed in 1903 and while it built and started up its first sawmill in Potlatch Town in 1906. By the time Rutledge Timber Company constructed and started up a sawmill at Coeur d'Alene in 1916, R.M. Weyerhaeuser was its president. And when the Clearwater Timber Company sawmill began operations in 1927 at Lewiston, J. P. Weyerhaeuser, Jr. was at the helm. The Lewiston sawmill was the biggest of the three, with a lumber production capacity of 400,000 board feet per eight-hour shift. It grew to operate 75 lumber dry kilns and 16 planer mills. Then in 1931, the three operations merged as Potlatch Forests, Inc., with Rudolph Weyerhaeuser as president.

Norval didn't see the impressive Lewiston mill very often, as that summer he and Burnell began falling and bucking big timber over to the east beyond Orofino in the vicinity of the town of Headquarters, which sat on the steep slopes off the North Fork of the Clearwater River.

The white pines were called "King Pine" and towered up to 200 ft. tall and were so dense that little light penetrated the forest floor. Western red cedar also was a significant species and some western hemlock was in the mix.

As experienced as he was, now Norval was in the big leagues. No mistakes allowed. The recent setback in the economy, more of a recession than the earlier Great Depression, had crippled the economy once again. There were many veteran loggers on the waiting list at Potlatch Forests. Burnell had assured the supervisors that his brother was a sure bet, which is what Norval turned out to be. The brothers bunked along with a dozen other men in one of the many rail cars that had been refurbished into comfortable-enough living quarters at one of the dozen logging camps. Two-tiered wooden bunks lined the outside walls. A kerosene lamp offered dim light and a cast iron stove in the middle of the room provided heat and a place to dry clothes.

The food was especially good in the camps: corned beef, ham, bacon, oysters, chicken, potatoes, fresh fruits and vegetables, biscuits, breads, milk, coffee and tea. Loggers ate an enormous amount of food,

The going was rough, but the food was great in the camps.

as many as 8,000 calories at a sitting in order to have the stamina for one 10-hour shift. Fallers and buckers could burn up to 12 calories a minute. When the food quality went down at a camp, the head count generally did as well.

Norval and Burnell formed a falling team as good as any in the camp. Their primary tool to tackle King Pine was the two-man crosscut saw, about eight feet in length with handles on each end. Some people called it a misery whip. Just as important to productivity were their springboards and two-sided axes. The men pierced either side of the tree a certain distance above ground and lodged in their springboards, on which they stood as they chopped and chiseled out the angled top cuts and undercuts on one side of the tree, the side toward which they wanted the tree to fall. Then they shared the big saw to make the back cut straight through the tree to nearly the point of the angle of the earlier cuts. Sometimes they had to work their way higher up the tree with the springboard to reach their cutting point; this meant standing on the springboard as they made another notch above them in the tree, then clinging to the tree with their cork boots as they stuck the springboard in that notch and again climbed on the springboard, until they reached their desired height. Sometimes they would have to do this a third time. Like the best of fallers, they would pound a stake a couple of inches into the ground where they planned to drop the top of their tree and further bury the stake in the earth. King Pine crackled and landed with a "whomp" that echoed throughout the slopes. Many a stake is still discovered in the Northwest where fallers such as Norval and Burnell hit their target.

Norval and Burnell brought plenty of other equipment to the timber stands, such as wedges for keeping the saw blade free, axe stones and an oil bottle, not to mention a lunch box when their locations were too remote to return to the cookhouse.

Then, usually assisted by a third man from the skidding team, they bucked or sawed the felled tree into 32 ft. and 40 ft. sawlog lengths. Felled timber on the steeper slopes always required teams of horses to skid out. Potlatch owned about 350 head of horses, each weighing 1600 pounds up to a ton. "Cat" tractors could skid out logs on more level terrain either to the diesel hoisting machines at the railroad loading points or to the flume loading points or to the landings where trucks were loaded with Loadmaster log loaders. Potlatch ran up to 200 trucks during the summer, hauling to the three area sawmills. The company operated 60 skidding tractors, a mix of Caterpillar, International Harvester and Allis Chalmers. And it operated 10 oil burning geared engines in its significant railroad operation.

The most important recent "discovery" was the bulldozer, which redefined the transportation infrastructure in the woods. With these they could more easily lay down skidding roads, truck roads and railroads. Mostly Isaacson, LeTourneau and Willamette-Hyster models, the bulldozer reduced the company's cost of road building by half.

Norval was witnessing and working in the middle of a transitory era for the Northwest logging industry. It still maintained many of the characteristics that had given it folklore status, such as the falling Norval and Burnell were doing and the small tools they were using, but now the industry welcomed new, mechanized technologies in skidding, loading and transportation. These new methods were not lost on Norval.

Even the corporate approach to land management was expanding, with selective-cutting of forests joining clear-cutting in the equation. For the first time Norval likely heard the description "Sustained Yield Forest Management," which Potlatch officials were saying was in sight. "The balance between growth and cutting of white pine forests will be reached in the near future," a Potlatch forester commented.

Something else Norval would have noticed was the use of wood waste for heat energy. The sawmill at Lewiston for example burned green hog fuel and shavings and generated 40 million pounds of steam each month. Potlatch also produced a product called Pres-To-Logs, a 4 inch by 12 inch long briquette fire log that was made by pressing dry wood waste that was originally green hog fuel from the sawmill that had been re-ground before running through a special hog fuel dryer and pressed into shape.

But what impressed Norval the most, and made a lasting impression, were the wages for his work.

"We made big money," Norval said. "We got $1.20 a thousand for falling and bucking big timber. We could make from $100 to $125 a week. That was unheard of in Michigan during those years."

The Morey brothers were piling up their wages and spreading some around.

"My brother bought a brand new Plymouth car with all the trinkets on it for just under $800," Norval said. "I had about the same amount of money as he did, and I sent my father $600. My father told me later that he had never seen that much money at one time in his life."

Norval's sister Lucille wasn't surprised that Norval sent the money home. To her it was another example of her older brother's giving ways.

"Nub looked after me my whole life," she said. "He was a good brother to me and like a second father to my children."

Loyal Morey may have used some of the money Norval sent home to buy a radio, as Lucille remembers their getting one at home in Winn about this time. It was the family's first opportunity to sit together and listen to the new soap operas, musical shows and the comedy series, Amos 'n' Andy, of which they had caught bits and pieces over the years.

Unlike the earlier radios of the neighbors, this one had a broadcast speaker. Loyal and Hazel also listened to the increasingly intense war news, most of which now focused on Hitler's hungry pursuit of world power. Three of their six sons were in the vicinity of draft age, and another was nearly there.

After the falling season ended, Norval remained in the Potlatch woods with 1,000 other workers to help in moving the felled logs to the various loading and transportation points, rebuilding river flumes and constructing camp facilities. It is very likely Norval operated some machinery at this point, either one of the Cat tractors or a Loadmaster loader. And it is possible he might have gotten a chance to drive one of the new bulldozers.

In the logging off-season Norval again found work as a laborer on a

Norval, above, and Burnell take turns posing during a break from falling duties.

fruit farm in eastern Washington. Then as warm weather approached in 1939, Norval and Burnell headed to Washington state and found employment as fallers for Weyerhaeuser Company, off the Chehalis River in the big Douglas fir country on the west side of the Cascades. Here Norval observed the newer diesel-powered methods of mountainous skyline logging, which included a metal tower yarder stabilized with guy lines extending from blocks and rings at the top of the tower to various stumps. Also from the top of the tower extended a long high (sky) line that connected to a distant stump or tree or both. Along this line ran the roller carriage from which dangled the chokers that men on the ground connected to the timber felled by Norval and Burnell and the hundreds of other fallers. The yarder by means of a turning drum elevated the logs into the air and pulled them in. For many years instead of a metal tower yarder the job used a tall tree, called a spar, at the top of which the various lines were run through mechanical blocks; a nearby steam donkey engine provided the pulling power on the lines. But Norval and Burnell's falling techniques and equipment hadn't changed from their work in Idaho; the misery whip still prevailed. Only now the Doug fir was fatter than the trees to the east.

Neither had the dangerous nature of their work diminished. Norval told of having to spend a few days in a medical facility receiving treatment for a leg wound. He never told how he sustained the injury; the crux of his story was about the man in the bed next to him who had severely broken his ankle on the job and been laid up with a cast. The man continued to complain that his foot didn't feel "right" inside the cast, and he could smell an obnoxious odor in there. The medical staff paid no heed and finally the man, as Norval observed, cut open the cast himself and his foot, blackened and full of infection, grossly separated itself from his leg.

After the falling season, Burnell went back to Idaho and Norval found work as a laborer on a fruit farm in Whittle, Washington, not far from Burnell in Idaho. Not surprisingly, when the falling season began to roll around in late spring, Burnell showed up at Norval's with the news that a faller could make even better wages in northern California.

It sounded good to Norval, who was keeping track of all the states he had visited during his young life. He would later boast that he had visited all but two of the 50 states in America by age 22.

When they arrived to apply for the job at McCloud River Lumber in McCloud, California, and informed the supervisor of their falling experience, they were quickly added to the roster, with only one warning: If their big ponderosa pine split when it hit the earth, they were fired.

From Robert E. Swanson's book, *Rhymes Of A Western Logger*:

A Logger's Ten Commandments

Never sit down at the table to eat where another should sit.
This is the cause for a battle, that man is just li'ble to quit.

Wander not into the cookhouse before the guthammer has rung;
Cooks, as a rule, swing a clever – they're bitter and flippant of tongue.

Grab as the food is passed by you; for service don't bother your mate.
Speed is the essence of manners – your saucer should rest on your plate.

Praise nothing that's new 'til it's proven, but wait for the super to praise;
Supers alone have the brain-power to merit a thing by its ways.

Of a man, you should speak as you find him, though others may brand him a cur;
It may be his good reputation has been marred by a slanderous slur.

Money when saved is a worry, so never your pleasure deprive;
Live for today and be happy, tomorrow may never arrive.

Be lavish when spending your money, as a cheapskate never be caught;

There's nothing so low as the logger who says he is broke – when he's not.

Lines are your friends if you know 'em but deadly as bullets in flight;
Give 'em respect and your distance, and never stand there in the bight.

Timber-r when falling, means danger; stand well up above in the clear.
Sharp lookout will cheat undertakers, who gloat on a widow's sad tear.

Care you should have in the summer – for fire in a forest is crime.
Fire can destroy in a minute the growth of a century's time.

Now these are the Sacred Commandments, the rules by which loggers abide;
Laws of a life in the forest – as true as the laws of the tide.
Break them and suffer, then, stranger – they're ancient, and proven, and tried.

McCloud River Lumber was settled on the southern slope of Mt. Shasta off the west side of the southern end of the Cascade Range, about midway between Yreka to the north and Redding to the south. Norval and Burnell worked mostly in the upper reaches of McCloud River, which was thickly timbered with vast stands of big yellow and sugar pine. McCloud had long been a true company town with everything in it owned by the lumber company and used exclusively by its employees. In addition to housing for its mill employees, the town included a theater, a dance hall, bank and hospital. The operation had gone through several ownership changes since its inception in the late 1800s and had a couple of sawmill sites. The sawmill that was running when Norval and Burnell arrived had been built 20 years earlier on the northeast edge of town and was one of the biggest sawmills ever to operate in the state. Daily production exceeded half a million board feet, even larger than the Potlatch sawmill at Lewiston.

McCloud River Lumber owned or controlled more than 600,000 acres of timberland, almost all of it east of town. It had an extensive railroad system running from the woods to the mill—even more progressive than the Potlatch operation. For decades, the company had maintained small portable log camps for the loggers. These camps constantly moved as they followed the harvest operations. But in recent years the company had transitioned to larger, permanent camps, with fallers like Norval and Burnell being transported to their cutting sites. Norval and Burnell worked out of the White Horse camp, about 30 miles northeast of Pondosa.

As he had seen throughout the Potlatch operations, Norval again observed the rumblings of big machinery in the McCloud woods. Though it was no longer commercially manufactured, several McGiffert loaders straddled the McCloud railroad tracks loading log cars. Nearly a thousand of these impressive, albeit somewhat awkward looking, machines had been manufactured from around 1900 to 1930. The entire machine sat on legs that rested on the ground on either side of the tracks. The boiler and spools were mounted on a platform that was elevated over the tracks. The McGiffert was self-propelled, as it had chain-driven drive axles that moved the machine along the rails. The wheels were retracted up against the bottom of the platform when the machine was set up to load cars. The McGiffert straddled the tracks and empty log cars were shoved underneath the loader, with logs loaded onto the cars by a boom off the one side of the loader.

Norval and Burnell weren't long on the job when they heard an older co-worker refer to a "famous" workers' strike of 30 years ago at McCloud River Lumber. When they found themselves sitting near one of the veteran timbermen at the town tavern, they asked him about it. He said he didn't participate in the strike himself, but he was around when it happened. "It was mostly Italians at the mill," he had said. "They had grievances." Italians comprised a large part of the work force back then. They claimed discrimination at the company store and said the company supervisors called them "Dagos" and "Wops." They said the company hadn't made good on a promise of a wage increase and they wanted a 25 cents per day hike. In 1909, the year the strike occurred, wages at the mill averaged $1.75. The strikers were even more concerned about the McCloud housing situation. Those who had purchased cabins on company-owned land claimed that the company refused to buy back the cabins for a fair price, meaning they were essentially stuck as employees of McCloud River Lumber.

About 700 men went on strike. A group of 200 attempted to hijack a train going to one of the logging sites in order to persuade loggers there to stop working. The strike was thwarted, however, when the sheriff of Siskiyou County and two-dozen armed deputies blocked the instigators from reaching the site. Two days later, the disgruntled strikers occupied one of McCloud's headquarter buildings. They said they would kill anyone who attempted to work. The sheriff again confronted them with his deputies, but withdrew due to the overwhelming numbers of strikers. The strikers then seized a powder house and gained access to a ton of dynamite owned by the company. They paraded through McCloud, cut telegraph wires, seized the lighting plant and put the whole town in darkness, including the hospital.

The governor of California, James Gillett, ordered the state militia to the site under the command of the adjutant general, Joseph Lauck. The militia approached by train at noon on June 3. Their presence enabled the mill to begin partial operations, but the strikers were still prevalent and meetings between the strikers and the company went nowhere. Then dozens of men from the Thiel Detective Service of San Francisco, led by noted "King of the Strikebreakers" James Farley, arrived on the scene. The sheriff arrested the three strike leaders. The situation grew even more bizarre.

The next day, at the urging of the governor, an Italian Consul named Salvatore Rocca and his attorney arrived by train where 500 strikers greeted them with shouts of "Vive Italia." Rocca met with the jailed strike leaders and company officials. He worked out a settlement, which called for the strikers to leave McCloud and for the company to purchase their cabins at a value determined by arbitration.

The strikers and their families sold about 200 cabins and departed McCloud. The troops and detectives withdrew as well. The strike officially ended on June 8. Now facing a labor shortage, McCloud River Lumber once again began hiring Italians.

Norval and Burnell could only shake their heads at the tale of the great strike at McCloud River Lumber. Personally, they couldn't have been happier with their wages. In fact the company had since earned a reputation for treating its employees well, which is why some people referred to it as "Mother McCloud."

Work was Monday through Saturday, with card playing being the favorite nighttime activity in the McCloud camps. If it was possible to get to town, the loggers spent Saturday night and holidays frequenting the theater or dance hall. Often, tailors visited the camps to display materials and take measurements for loggers' clothing. The tailors brought whiskey with them as a courtesy and were likely to have shared some lively times with Norval and his brother. Norval made a few extra dollars by giving haircuts to fellow loggers. Missionaries sometimes visited the camps as well.

But Norval's great adventure in the Northwest was nearly over, though never to be forgotten. In 1939, Germany had invaded Poland, prompting Britain and France to declare war on Germany. Then Germany invaded France in May 1940 and the Battle of Britain commenced. The writing was on the wall. The U.S. would soon enter the war. President Roosevelt called for a draft of men 21 years and older. Burnell registered and went to Cottonwood, Idaho to be with his girlfriend Clara until he got the call from the Army. This would come in the spring of 1941.

Norval went back home to Michigan and registered for the draft. For the next few months, he helped Loyal and Hazel on the farm while waiting for his number to be called. He had to keep waiting.

"My brother was one of the first ones to be drafted," Norval said. "But I was never called into the Army until pretty near two years later. While I was waiting to get in the Army, I went to Detroit and got a job in a defense plant, and worked there until I was drafted."

Norval wasn't in Detroit long when he received tragic news. His Uncle Clell Morey, the man who had enticed Burnell to Idaho, leading to Norval's migration west as well, and with whom Norval and Burnell had enjoyed many festive times, was dead. After spending a Labor Day holiday in Lewiston, Clell and three of his co-workers died in the early morning hours of September 2, 1941 when their car ran off the road, crashed and over-turned in a swampy pond, killing all of the men. The accident occurred just inside the town limits of Weippe, which

Norval left the farm to work in Detroit defense plants.

was a little southeast of Orofino. Clell, who wasn't driving, and his three friends were returning to their camp. Clell was just shy of 40 years old. Burnell, who was still in Idaho, chaperoned the body back east to Winn, where Clell was buried in Union Cemetery. Norval

The local newspaper caught Norval, far right, registering for the draft, and not looking real excited about it.

attended the service, which was held in the front room of the Morey cabin. More than one family member commented at the tragic irony of Clell being killed in this manner when for years he had worked as a river jammer, the most dangerous job in the woods. Crossed axes were etched into Clell's headstone.

By now in Winn, nearly everyone was hooked up with telephone service. The Morey family shared a party line with their neighbors, including long-time friends, the Giffords, whose matriarch, Susie, was Hazel Morey's best friend. The two women spent portions of every day chatting with each other. Often, when she wasn't speaking to Susie, Hazel would pick up the phone just to listen to what others had to say. "I don't know if she had breathing problems or not, but my grandmother breathed heavily," said Norval's son, Lon Morey. "When she was listening in, you could always hear her breathing. My dad would say, 'Hazel!' and she would hang up."

In Detroit, the big automakers Chrysler, GM and Ford were already beginning construction to convert to military production when Japan attacked Pearl Harbor and the U.S. entered the war in December, 1941.

Norval was one of 350,000 people who moved to Detroit by the end of 1942. The hopeful came in droves—women who'd never worked, careworn farmers, unemployed immigrants, and 60,000 African Americans, mostly from the South, each one wanting to latch on to a good paying defense job after 11 long years of Depression, recession and repression. By the end of 1942, automobile production had totally ceased. Detroit became known as the "Arsenal of Democracy." Chrysler's tank plant opened in 1941. Ford's Willow Run B-24 Liberator factory opened in 1942. Ford also produced the 4x4 Jeep. GM produced armored cars, amphibious vehicles, a range of tanks, aircraft engines and propellers at its plants. Roosevelt appointed GM president William Knudsen as head of Wartime Production. Oldsmobile, a division of GM, manufactured artillery shells.

Norval's sister, Lucille, recollected that Norval might have worked at one of the GM plants, though Norval's longtime right hand man at Morbark, Larry Burkholder, said it could have been the Willow Run plant. Burkholder was certain that Norval operated an overhead crane wherever he was in Detroit. And one reason Burkholder said Norval may have been at the Ford plant was because Norval through the years always expressed admiration for the disciplined, assembly line techniques implemented at Ford factories.

Detroit became a place of cultural upheaval. So many workers all coming in at once had overwhelmed city services and snarled traffic. Interstate 90 was built specifically to move people in and out of Ford's

Willow Run facility, where early production scheduling was so chaotic a local nickname for the plant was "Will It Run."

The government began throwing up dormitories and trailer parks in record time to house them all. At one government-built housing complex at the Ford plant at Willow Run, 15,000 workers were housed on site. A website devoted to wartime defense production in Detroit's automobile plants run by the Michigan Department of Natural Resources and the Michigan Historical Museum chronicles the daily lives of those who worked in the massive plants. A new two bedroom unit rented for about $25 a month. It was comfortable and clean, but the walls were paper thin. If somebody was cooking onions, the immediate neighbors and several down the line could smell them. The apartments were built in a row with shared walls and they all looked alike. It wasn't unusual for new residents to get off the bus at the wrong stop, and encounter trouble finding their units

The crush of people enhanced racial tension and when African Americans were allowed to integrate factory housing communities, violence erupted. The most severe incident was in June of 1943. Some 1,800 people were arrested, 600 were injured and 45 were killed. Federal troops were called in to calm the city.

Norval would take several lessons from his Detroit experience. One was management-to-employee relations, and the importance of maintaining communication with employees. The other was big-time manufacturing, where urgency was the code word, production schedules paramount and innovations unleashed and tested on a daily basis.

The Army finally called him up in September of 1942 and he immediately left Michigan for infantry training.

It would be years before Norval put the lessons he learned at the Detroit defense plants in motion at his own business. He had other matters to attend to. He was in the Army now.

TWO

Mountains
Northern Italy
October, 1944

T*he push was on to the Alps, but Staff Sergeant Norval Morey, who didn't know much about geography, knew the Alps were still a long way away—maybe 100 more Italian mountains and towns away, maybe more than that. What he knew was that no matter how many mountains and towns were ahead, he, his squad, his platoon, his company, his regiment, his 88th Infantry Division, his Fifth Army, his United States Army, would have to capture them all from an enemy which didn't even live there. The Italian military had long ago thrown in the towel. The German military was the defender, and it was becoming increasingly obvious to the German soldier, with each Italian mountain and town that he retreated from, that the war would be lost, probably along with his life, which made him desperate, fanatical and highly dangerous to Norval Morey.*

Norval's unit had taken another mountain, this time without much opposition, but they weren't finished digging their foxholes when the enemy helmets appeared through the swirling clouds. Everybody seemed to be moving in slow motion. Mud up to the knees and pelting rain bogged down the entire battle. Artillery fired by both sides decimated the ranks. The screams of men bounced off the mountain. German potato mashers and U.S. hand grenades bypassed each other in the air. Machine gun fire riddled the rocky terrain. Rifle shots came in bunches, then sporadically, then it was quiet. The enemy disappeared back into the clouds. Norval bet, and he was a betting man, that the enemy would make it all the way up next time—hand-to-hand combat, bayonets, knives, pistols.

Norval tried to leave that thought behind and went to work on his foxhole again. He took a drink of water from his canteen and felt something slippery run down his throat. Earlier that day he had scooped up some water at the bottom of another foxhole into his canteen. Now he poured out some of the contents—worms, bugs, and some junk he couldn't identify. He looked at it a moment and winced. "I'd trade places with Burnell in a heartbeat," he thought. "Well, maybe not," he thought again. The picture of sitting in a tank, straight across from a German Panzer, as his brother Burnell probably was doing at that moment...Norval took another swig, swallowed down the liquid as best he could and spat out the remainder.

He was called back to the First Lieutenant, who was still shaking over the battle just ensued. The lieutenant was new to the job, having just arrived with a company of replacements. His hands shook as he revealed a roughly sketched map to Norval. "The Commander wants to send out three squads on reconnaissance," he said. "You're to move down this trail and at this point sweep west for 200 yards. If it's clear, you continue to circle back. If you engage, maintain your position and you'll receive direct support. We'll hear you."

The lieutenant's voice didn't make it sound like an order. He knew Norval had been on the front lines for six months. He looked at Norval for Norval's approval of the plan, which Norval knew the lieutenant had recited word for word from the commander. Norval didn't approve the plan, but he knew it was out of the lieutenant's hands and it wasn't worth the hassle to disagree.

The way Norval saw it, if Norval took his squad where the plan said to go, they would be pinched on two sides as soon they began to sweep and their only alternatives would be to shoot it out against a greater force, while waiting for "direct support," or haul ass back up the hill while the enemy shot them in the back.

Norval saluted the lieutenant. The weather had worsened if that was possible. Darkness encompassed the mountain. He rounded up his squad, a dozen soldiers. This was new business for about eight of them. He had recruited them at base camp to replace the killed and wounded. That was how it worked.

But not this time, he thought. No walking into an obvious firefight this time. No young dead soldiers on his hands. No dead Norval Morey either. He directed the squad down the trail, through the mud and rain and clouds, but instead of sweeping through the brush he told them to take a knee and maintain silence. He and his squad remained where they were for half an hour; then they retraced their steps back up to their foxholes. He reported to the lieutenant that there was nothing to report, but he was certain the enemy was over there somewhere.

The U.S. Army didn't call Norval's number until September 23, 1942. He had made good money in Detroit. He wasn't chomping at the bit to do his time in the service, but the wait was frustrating and he was ready to get on with it. What he got first was a year and a half of training with the 89th Infantry Division, starting with desert and mountain training near Colorado Springs and Lake George, Colorado, stationed at Fort Carson; followed by exercises in the swampy, gumbo terrain of Louisiana, stationed at Camp Polk; then the division headed in late January 1944 to Camp Roberts

Norval could be mischievous at times, even in the military. But he would prove himself in the battlefield.

in the coastal range of California for extensive training in mountainous country thickly covered by almost impenetrable brush—terrain comparable it was said to the mountains of northern Italy and the islands of the southwest Pacific.

The extremely difficult maneuvers in California extended into

April, when the announcement came that the 89th would be reorganized and many of its troops moved out either as replacements overseas or to other outfits in the states. But before any of that happened, the troops received word that they would be receiving a furlough.

"They pulled us all into a tent camp and said they were giving everybody a ten day furlough," Norval recalled. "I waited for a couple of weeks and finally my turn came to go on the furlough."

Norval had made contact with a solider who was also from near Winn, Michigan and they decided to catch a train back home. They boarded a cattle car train but a day into the ride knew they had gotten themselves into a pickle.

"This kind of train didn't have much priority on the railroad tracks," Norval said. "Cargo and troop trains moved ahead of them. We had ten days to go home and be back. We knew it was very unlikely we would have more than a day or two at home at this rate."

They had even less time. It took them five days to reach Lansing, Michigan. "In order to be back on time, we would have had to catch the next train the next morning for California."

Norval and his friend took matters into their own hands, another early indicator of Norval's independent mindset when he felt what he was doing made sense to him. They decided to take their 10 day furlough "at home" and suffer the consequences when they returned to camp. They figured they were about to be shipped overseas anyway, so why rush it. They hitchhiked from Lansing to Winn. Norval spent a relaxing, enjoyable 10 days at home, catching up with the family and old friends, and marching to his own schedule.

He also resumed his steadily deepening acquaintance with a young lady from the area named Phyllis Barrett. She had been rooming with Norval's sister, Lucille, when Norval met her on his first furlough in May 1943 and they went out on a couple of dates, and continued to date when Norval received another furlough in September 1943.

Now after ten days at home in April 1944, Norval bid Phyllis farewell, rendezvoused with his solider friend and boarded a train and headed back to California.

"Of course the minute we got there, we were pulled into the Colonel's office and were court-martialed for being AWOL," Norval said. "About all they did was fine us. If I remember right it was $200. If you didn't have the money, they just took it out of your pay."

In a few days Norval was on another train bound for Baltimore, Maryland where he would be shipped abroad. "It took two or three weeks there to get everybody sorted out," Norval said. "About all there was to do was gamble and, if we made any money, go to Washington. Well I always did quite well in a poker game and crap game in the Army and I made plenty of money, so we went to Washington about every other day."

Norval was shipped overseas in June 1944.

According to a special dates book kept by Norval's mom, Hazel, Norval called home on June 2, 1944 a few days before shipping out. Certainly they must have talked about the recent passing of Norval's grandfather, Loren Morey, who had suffered a heart attack and died at his home on May 27. Loren had been in ill health for the past year. Loren had always been extremely helpful to Norval's dad and the Morey boys with building and carpentry work on the farm. Norval felt fortunate that he had been able to visit his grandfather during his recent furlough. Loren had lived alone since Norval's grandmother, Emma Jane, had died after a long illness way back when Norval was 10 years old. Now both of his grandparents were buried in Union Cemetery in nearby Blanchard, along with Loren's parents, Israel and Mary Ann, and Emma Jane's father, Christian Uebele, and two of Emma Jane's sisters.

Then they loaded Norval and the troops on trucks and headed for the shipyard. Here several troops were immersed in a crap game on a big sheet of canvas. Norval joined them with $100 in his pocket and proceeded to lose it all.

"So when I got on the ship as far as I knew I had an Indian Head penny in a little case attached to my dog tags. So I thought I had one cent when I got on the ship, until the next day when I changed my pants and I discovered a dime in the pocket. So actually I had 11 cents."

Norval was on a ship to North Africa when Allied forces invaded Normandy, France and as Allied armies captured and moved through Rome, Italy. Norval's brother, Burnell, participated in the Normandy invasion as a technical sergeant in the 745th Tank Battalion.

At North Africa, Norval was put on the Queen Elizabeth bound for Naples, Italy. "There were a lot of Army nationalities on the ship, soldiers from South America, Africa, all over the world. We were a few days getting there; the Queen Elizabeth was a big ship, but not a very fast one.

"We pulled into Naples and it was completely destroyed. The harbor was there but the city had been shelled from the ocean and bombed with airplanes. There were kids running around starving to death. The city was unbelievable."

Norval went to a huge replacements camp on a dairy farm where he would eventually be assigned his outfit and trucked out. He had only been there two days when he and two others decided to visit a little nearby town and score some booze. "We knew we weren't supposed to go until we had a pass, but we didn't figure we'd get caught," Norval said. "What we didn't realize was that there was nobody in that area with OD clothes on that had a pass."

The MP's spotted them in no time, took them back to camp and put them in a barbed wire pen along with about 50 other wayward troops. Norval was court-martialed yet again and fined. "Colonel (James) Fry was the commanding officer there," Norval said. "He made us stand at attention out there for at least two or three hours in about 105 degree temperatures while he went through the court-martial. What they were really doing was putting on a show for new recruits that were just coming in for replacements." Col. Fry was the commander of the 350th infantry regiment of the 88th division.

"In a day or two we were sent right to the front lines," Norval recalled. "They gave me a pack and a rifle with a bunch of other fellows and took us to join the 88th (Infantry) Division."

The 88th was composed primarily of drafted men, causing some initial apprehension about their capabilities in combat. Instead the division's fighting acumen would become legendary and during the war the 88th was honored with the nickname, Blue Devils. It had already proven itself before Norval's arrival.

The primary regiments of the 88th division were the 349th, 350th and 351th. Norval appears to have reached the outfit shortly after it had captured Rome as well as some territory north of Rome. He encountered battle-hardened young men.

In the previous month the 88th had participated in the assault of the Gustav Line, which was the German line that ran across Italy from just north of where the Garigliano River flows into the Tyrrhenian Sea of the Mediterranean in the west, through the Apennine Mountains to the mouth of the Sangro River on the Adriatic coast in the east. The center of the line crossed the main route north to Rome, Highway 6, which followed the Liri Valley. The Gustav line was heavily fortified with gun pits, concrete bunkers, turreted machine-gun emplacements, barbed-wire and minefields.

Earlier, in a strategic move back on January 22, elements of the U.S. Fifth Army had landed 50 miles northwest of the Gustav Line at Anzio Beach. Anzio was selected because it was considered the best site within striking distance of Rome, which was only 35 miles to the north, but still within range of Allied aircraft operating from Naples to the south. The landing, which covered a 15 mile stretch of beach, encountered minimal resistance and by midnight the allies had 36,000 soldiers ashore. Tens of thousands of men and vast amounts of armor and equipment continued to come in as the inland perimeter was expanded. Eventually the beachhead advance was halted, and troops settled in for four months of German ground, air and artillery attacks.

Inland to the southeast, the 88th had been in the front line opposite the German Gustav Line, mainly improving defensive positions while firing artillery at German positions. Then on May 11 the entire Allied inland front, including Americans, Englishmen, Frenchmen, Canadians and Poles, and including the 88th division, began a massive night assault on the Gustav Line. The goal was to break through the line and beat back the enemy until linking up with the coastal Allied forces at Anzio as they broke out of the beachhead. During the 88th assault, Staff Sergeant Charles Shea of the 350th regiment destroyed three enemy machine guns while inflicting severe casualties in capturing the key terrain of Mt. Damiano and became the first Blue Devil to receive the Medal of Honor. Meanwhile the 351st took Santa Maria Infante following a great battle. The Allied lines were forcing the stubborn foe off the Gustav Line. The 88th Division doggedly pursued the withdrawing Germans until on May 29 it made contact with Allied units successfully breaking out of Anzio to the west, in effect now extending the Allied line across all of Italy.

The division entered Rome on June 4, working through steady enemy fire and under harassment from snipers. Despite the continuing warfare, civilians left their homes to greet the first troops. By noon of June 5 the celebration in Rome was at its zenith with singing and dancing in the streets, and flowers and kisses filling the air. The capture of Rome had come with a high price. Since the assault on the Gustav Line began back on May 11, the Fifth Army, of which the 88th was a part, had suffered 17,931 American casualties including 3,145 killed. German losses were 38,000 and another 17,000 prisoners of war.

For the next three days the 88th advanced north of Rome about 40 miles. They were then trucked 50 miles out of the line down to Albano, about 15 miles southeast of Rome, over some of the very same turf the 88th had fought over and won in the past two weeks. This was most likely where Norval joined the outfit. For the first time the soldiers would get to enjoy the celebration of taking Rome as they went into a week long rest period from June 14-18. Soldiers made the most of a nearby lake and its beach, meditated in shower facilities and relished the feel of newly issued clothing. Passes were issued to visit Rome, and the men took in the movies and other entertainment befitting the conquering Blue Devils. Newcomer Norval recalled that he sold cigarettes and various other items on the black market to gather spending money and would be able to do this in many of the towns the regiment captured.

Norval wasn't much for writing, but he took advantage of the break to write his mother. He told her not to allow his younger brother, Milford, to enlist in the Army. Milford had only recently turned 18 and Norval knew he was anxious to enter the war. Two sons in the war were enough, Norval said, referring to himself and his older brother Burnell with the 745th Tank Battalion. Norval figured Burnell had even rougher days ahead of him in France and Germany, and Norval, hearing some of the stories his new comrades were telling, certainly didn't see the fighting letting up anytime soon in Italy. Norval advised Milford to take care of the home front for the sake of their parents. But Milford didn't adhere to it. He enlisted in the Army only a short time later on July 29. Another brother, Ralph, had already been in and out of the Army. Ralph had entered the Army in October 1942 and been promoted to corporal, only to be hampered with foot ailments and was medically discharged in October 1943.

Meanwhile Norval received a lot of letters himself, many of them from Phyllis, the girl he had dated during furloughs back home. They had hit it off, but home and Phyllis seemed a long way away to Norval. He was heading in the wrong direction.

Letters also came from his sister Mildred, full of prayer for Norval's well-being. Norval's other sister, Lucille, recalled, "My sister was the one who always prayed for the rest of us. She got saved when she was 12 years old and was firm in her conviction. I can still see her down on her knees praying."

Rest period for the 88th Infantry Division passed all too quickly, as the regiments entered several days of extensive training, with emphasis on firing arms, including the M-1 rifle, carbines, rifle grenades and bazookas. Then it was time to load up again for Tarquinia, some 60 miles north of Rome. There, Lt. Gen. Mark Clark, Fifth Army Commander, told them during an awards ceremony, "The thrill of victory is in the air." Norval and the troops participated in recreational activities following the ceremony, including swimming and splashing about in the Tyrrhenian Sea.

Victory may have been in the air, but Norval and the 88th were about to experience 10 months of nearly constant combat. Taking out enemy machine guns and dodging hand grenades would become a way of life as the 88th Division chased the Germans in the mud and rocks up and over endless Italian mountains and hills and through rain-drenched town after town.

The division advanced north to Pomarance and participated in stiff combat with the Germans before crossing the Era River near Cipriano. This most likely was Norval's initiation to combat. It took three weeks for the division to fight its way through 15 miles of rugged, hilly terrain and mountain towns, encountering heavy artillery and mortar fire, thick mine fields and strongly held German positions. One-hundred-forty soliders in the 350th regiment were killed and 540 wounded. The unit went into bivouac near Villamagna for two weeks, conducting extensive training in river crossing, holding platoon and squad management sessions and also rebuilding the pack mule companies. The 350th regiment pack mule company consisted of four sections of 60 mules each divided into four squads of fifteen mules.

Norval realized these were his living conditions until the end of the war. But he felt like he was prepared. "I was fairly well trained to stand the living conditions. I had been on maneuvers for six or seven months in the United States that I hadn't slept in a bed. I knew how to live outdoors. I was in good physical condition and pretty tough, so I figured I could be as good a soldier as anybody else. And I would do whatever they told me to do and hope the war would be over soon. We had a lot of hard training in the United States and when we did go overseas I believe I was as ready as you can get in that short a time for frontline combat.

"Not that you're trained so much for fighting a war, but you are for the living conditions. Sometimes we would be sleeping in foxholes for a week or 10 days at a time. It seemed like it never quit raining in the summertime or in the fall and spring, and in the winter it was very cold and it wasn't unusual to be in a foxhole when it was below zero. So you had to be in condition and trained to survive that kind of living condition."

The Allied advance in France was receiving most of the attention. Several U.S. infantry divisions in Italy were moved to the France sector, weakening somewhat the total force of the Fifth and Eighth armies continuing the war in Italy. This meant even tougher fighting for Norval and the 88th against a foe whose back was inching ever closer against the wall and becoming increasingly desperate. The next major objective was to push to the Arno River.

The 88th advanced toward the mountain city of Volterra, and it took a daylong battle to reach the entrance to the city. It took several days to overcome severe opposition along the ridges and capture Laiatico. One by one the mountain towns fell to the U.S., almost all of them ferociously defended by the Germans who weren't hesitant to counterattack their pursuers. U.S. casualties mounted in staggering proportions. By mid-September the division camped near Florence, and then advanced north toward the German defensive position known as the Gothic Line.

"I wasn't in combat a very short time till I realized that it was much better to be a non-commissioned officer, a sergeant, than it was to be a private," Norval said. "A lot of times the orders were to 'take this house or that one' and instead of giving the orders I was sticking my neck out too often. It appeared to me, you might not last too long. So I was there only a short time and they made me a platoon sergeant. The reason you could jump from private to possibly platoon sergeant was not because I was so good, but because of the shortage of people with any experience in combat. If you had a month of combat experience, you were an old-timer."

Not only non-commissioned officers but also commissioned officers such as lieutenants and captains came to Norval for advice when they came on the front lines.

"I spent most of the time on the front lines," Norval said. "When we weren't on the front lines we were back getting replacements to go up again. Many times you would start out with 15 or 20 men in your platoon and wind up with four or five. Then you'd come back and get replacements and do the same thing over again.

"Leading men in the Army sometimes meant yelling loud and being mean. It wasn't the kind of a job I liked, and I was happy when the whole thing was over and we got on the ship in Rome to come home."

The 88th was about to experience its bloodiest combat of the war in severe mountain terrain. The division captured several mountain points, each time encountering groups of enemy dug in and fighting hard before withdrawing to the next defendable feature and the process would start all over again. In the battle for Mt. Acuto, a fellow Michigander of Norval's, Capt. Thomas Cussans of Flint, took over for his fallen commander and led his company's charge up the heights in the face of heavy enemy fire, routing the German defenders.

Fog, rain and mud became even more severe as the 349th took Mt. Pratolungo, and as the 351st captured Castel del Rio, Mt. Guasteto and Mt. Capello. The battle for Capello lasted two days and called for close range combat, including the use of the bayonet. It would get even worse for the 350th regiment at Mt. Battaglia, a perfect high ground 11 miles from the Po Valley.

Norval shared only a few short war stories with only a few close friends and relatives, and when he told them he never identified locations by name or battles by dates. A few stories he told seemed to be set during the fight for Mt. Battaglia. One of his humorous stories was as the regiment was occupying the heights, which it did with almost no opposition. As he walked with fellow troops toward the high ground one of the commanders pulled along side in his jeep, stopped and exchanged light conversation with the soldiers as they passed by. Norval commented to a nearby private that the commander's jeep contained a nice looking sleeping bag. That night Norval wrapped himself in the same sleeping bag in his foxhole.

There would be no more moments of comic relief for the next

seven days and nights, as the Germans constantly attacked the Americans entrenched around the shattered remains of a castle. Clouds hugged the mountaintop, concealing advancing Germans until they were within a few yards of the defenders. Hand-to-hand combat ensued when the Germans briefly took the highest point, only to see the Americans rally and re-take it, leaving German dead inside the castle foundations. German artillery supported the Kraut troops, who came several times with flamethrowers. U.S. troops constantly dealt with mud in their firearms, but their hand grenades successfully beat back the attackers. Meanwhile litter bearers regularly evacuated the casualties out of the area despite constant artillery and mortar barrages. Pack mule trains continued to bring supplies to the soldiers, but at times ammunition supply became low and when the men exhausted their hand grenades, they resorted to throwing rocks at the oncoming enemy.

Norval spoke of being burrowed into a mountainside for several days. He recalled when he shared a foxhole with a "kid" as he called him. They hadn't slept for a couple of days and Norval took watch as the kid dozed off. But when it came Norval's turn to sleep, as Norval recalled, "I didn't trust this kid to stay awake. And the enemy was very close." But Norval did fall asleep and when he awoke the end of a German rifle barrel was entering the foxhole.

Norval didn't complete the story. But apparently the kid had fallen asleep, and when Norval awoke a fight ensued and Norval killed the enemy intruder. Craig Price, who worked at Morbark Industries, was a paramedic and was at Norval's side late in Norval's life as he battled illness, said Norval often didn't finish his combat stories. "He would tell it to a certain point and you were waiting for him to finish it," Price said. "But then he would get this look on his face. You could tell he didn't want to remember and he'd get up and walk away. I kind of surmised that the kid might not have come out of that battle alive."

Norval also recalled to his stepdaughter Michelle White when during a lull in the battle a young soldier in his unit "went insane," jumped out of his foxhole and ran into an opening in plain view of the Germans. The soldier was shouting and pleading to God to help him. Norval and the other men in the unit desperately called for him to come back, but enemy fire killed him. "I think dad soured on religion based on that experience, even though I don't think he came from a particularly religious family," Michelle said.

During this same period Norval recalled a night when several members in his squad became anxious and panicky thinking they heard the enemy coming toward them from a certain direction. Norval tried to calm down his troops. "That's not what's happening. They're not coming in," Norval said. He led the squad to a small area and told them "we're going to have our own little battle." He ordered them to start shooting blindly in one direction and soon they heard the enemy's movement, which revealed that an attack was not immediately forthcoming. Norval's troops breathed easier for the moment.

Norval was very much about surviving the war. "I want to sleep in a real bed one more time," he would say. In such combat the lives of he and his men frequently hung in the balance, but he wanted at least a fighting chance. He told of receiving an order to take his squad on a patrol that to him seemed fatally doomed. He led them away from base camp and then ordered them to park themselves. After a while he and his men returned to camp with no action or sighting to report.

The 88th held Mt. Battaglia and the surrounding hills, but the 350th regiment suffered 50 percent casualties. Still the 88th division pushed on, with Mt. Grande as the next key target. En route they captured Mt. Cerrere, Del Chin, Di Sotto, Di Sopra, and took Mt. Grande on October 20 following a major battle. From here on a clear day they could view the Po Valley and the highway to Bologna. Camped in the vicinity of Mt. Grande for the next several weeks, the soldiers received passes into Florence. Long showers and a change of clothing prepared the men for their visit to the town theaters.

By December 1944 the troops were only 11 miles from Bologna—the key to the Po Valley. Here they remained through the remainder of the year. Snow blanketed the entire front on Christmas Day.

The first three months of 1945 came with patrol clashes, ambush raids, artillery fire and the other painful incidents of war to which the

Norval, far right, as a combat squad leader constantly had the tragic duty of rounding up replacements to fill the holes created by those who were killed in combat.

88th had grown to accept as part of their daily existence. In April 1945 the 88th began its assault on Monterumici Hill, the key to the entire enemy defense line before Bologna. Despite the fury of artillery, mortars, tanks and machine guns directed at Monterumici Hill, the German defenders emerged with some of their toughest resistance of the war. U.S. soldiers advanced up the slopes but immediately encountered enemy fire. Casualties were sustained when men dove into the shelter of nearby foxholes, only to plunge right into booby traps. As soon as the U.S. troops took the hill, they began pursuit of the retreating Germans and chased them across the Po River. After a long march the division captured Ostiglia, then took Verona to split the German forces in half, followed by the capture of Vicenza with bitter house-to-house fighting.

Entire German units began to surrender now but the 88th still encountered resistance as it rolled through S. Pietro in Gu. More and more the U.S. troops witnessed Italian civilians physically bashing German troops, some of the incidents extremely gruesome. It became well known that Germans soldiers would happily surrender to American soldiers, but that they would fight fanatically against the local partisans.

The 88th had fought furiously into the Po Valley and now stood at the foothills of the mighty snow-covered Alps on a land that had never seen a foreign soldier move the complete length of the Italian Peninsula, until now.

Then it was over, at least in Europe. Word reached the division on May 2, 1945 that the German armies had surrendered unconditionally. Two days later a few miles south of Brenner Pass, advance patrols of the 349th regiment of the 88th division connected with Allied forces moving south from Germany, making the European and Mediterranean fronts one unbroken line.

During the past 16 days, since its jumpoff against Monterumici on the heights south of Bologna, the 88th had conquered 305 miles, destroyed six Nazi divisions and captured 35,000 enemy soldiers. In 344 days of combat in Italy, the 88th Infantry Division lost 2,298 men killed in action and 9,225 wounded. The Fifth Army, which included the 88th division among others, in 602 days of combat had suffered 109,642 American casualties, of which 19,475 had been killed in action.

But Norval's fighting didn't appear to be finished. His outfit was transported to Rome to start training for action in the Pacific against the Japanese. The U.S. was planning to invade southernmost Japan in October and 2.3 million fanatical Japanese troops were preparing to defend the homeland to the last man. Another U.S. invasion nearer Tokyo would follow in early spring. Estimates of Allied casualties varied dramatically, up to 4 million, of which the dead count could reach 800,000.

"But before they shipped us down there, we dropped the Atomic bomb and the war was over in Japan," Norval said. "So I was shipped back to the United States."

The U.S. dropped two bombs, the first on Hiroshima on August 6, and the second one on Nagasaki on August 9. Japan surrendered on August 15.

Norval's stepdaughter, Michelle White, said Norval recalled to her that he was one of only two original members of his company to survive the war. Norval referred to the other survivor only as "Bob, from Maine."

Norval's joy of returning home was pierced with the heartbreaking news that his younger brother Milford was reported missing in action. Milford had not wanted to miss the war and he signed on at age 18 in July 1944. He had been able to return home on furlough from his camp in Texas during Christmas, before shipping overseas during the first week in January of 1945. He landed in France and joined the 3rd Infantry Division of the 7th Army. The 3rd was one of the most combat-experienced units in the Army, having participated in the invasions and battles of North Africa and Italy before moving to the war in France in August 1944. Milford had hit the ground running when he joined Company I of the 15th regiment of the 3rd Division in January. The unit was embroiled in the notorious battle of the Colmar Pocket on the French side of the France-German border.

When Milford arrived, the unit posed a front in the Vosges Mountains. Snow, strong icy winds and minus ten degree temperatures permeated the grounds. The unit had painted all of its armor and vehicles combat white. Probably about the time Milford arrived the 15th infantry crossed the Ill River and seized a strategic bridgehead around Maison Rouge. They then pushed through Riedwihr encountering small-arms, machine gun, tank and mortar fire along the way. In this vicinity, near Holtzwihr, one of Milford's fellow 15th regiment troopers, Second Lt. Audie Murphy, a commander of Company B, nearly single-handedly overcame six German tanks and scores of German infantry attacking his company. Mur-

Norval's young brother, Milford, entered the war despite Norval's pleadings, and was killed.

phy ordered his troops back to a position in the woods and then gave fire directions to his artillery by telephone. When a U.S. tank destroyer behind him received a direct hit and began to burn, Murphy climbed on it and began employing its .50 caliber machine gun against the enemy. He was alone and exposed to German fire from three sides. He killed dozens of Germans as they tried to approach him. Twice his tank destroyer was hit by artillery fire. His clothing was torn and riddled by flying shell fragments. Bullets ricocheted off the tank as the enemy concentrated its fury of fire on Murphy. German infantrymen got to within 10 yards of Murphy before he cut them down. After his ammunition ran out, and wounded in the leg, Murphy returned to his company and organized a counterattack, which forced the Germans to withdraw. Murphy killed or wounded 50 Germans. He received the Congressional Medal of Honor. Murphy became a movie star after the war and would play himself in the movie, "To Hell and Back."

Milford's unit continued the advance into the Niederwald woods, engaged the enemy in a firefight, killing many and taking 16 prisoners. Into early February Milford's unit steadily advanced until the 3rd Division had taken Neuf-Brisach and Colmar and isolated the pocket from the Rhine River.

The 3rd Division continued its assault on the German Siegfried Line. Milford's 15th regiment took Walshausen and Winzeln by March 21, and soon reached Nunschweiler, then took Kaiserslautern, and crossed the Rhine River on March 26. Resistance was sharp but the unit continued to capture town after town, before crossing the Main River at Worth, southeast of Frankfurt, on March 30.

The 15th ran into a fight southwest of Weibersbrunn, a little village hidden in a dense wooden area, but Milford's Company I helped to capture it and 25 prisoners; then it won a major battle at Rieneck near the Sinn River.

It may have been somewhere in the advance toward Bad-Neustadt that Milford was killed by artillery fire, as all highways were blasted by U.S. artillery and air support in the effort to stall the retreating Germans. He was reported missing in action on April 8, and three months later he was declared to have perished on that day. Norval's fear had come true. Milford, like many late sign-ups who didn't want to miss the war, was cast into a meat-grinder as the war ground to a close. Milford initially was buried in the Lorraine-American Cemetery in Saint-Avold, northeast France, with thousands of other U.S. soldiers. His personal effects were returned home in March 1947. His body would come home in due course. Milford Morey was one of 51 soldiers from Isabella County who were killed in World War II.

Like she had done for Norval, sister Mildred had written frequently to Milford and was overjoyed to receive a very special letter in return. Sister Lucille recalled, "She told me that right after Milford got overseas, she got a letter from him that he had accepted Jesus as his savior."

Norval was relieved that his older brother and lumberjack partner Burnell had survived. Burnell had gone overseas in August 1943 as a technical sergeant with the 745th Tank Battalion. He had come in with the battalion at Normany on D-Day June 6, and the battalion proceeded to support the 1st Infantry Division in the breakout of Normandy. Burnell would eventually command a tank platoon as it raced northeast across France, at one point covering 156 miles in just over 24 hours. His son, Jerry Morey, said that his father carried a sawed off Browning 12 gauge shotgun with him inside the tank, for when the enemy would jump on the tank and open the hatch to throw in hand grenades. "When they opened it up, he let it go," Jerry said. The shotgun saved Burnell's life at least a couple of times.

Burnell's battalion reached the outskirts of Aachen, Germany by September 11, 1944 and was engaged in tough fighting for the next three months, helping the 1st Infantry Division take Aachen and clear the Hurtgen Forest. On December 16 in the vicinity of Hergenrath, Belgium, the 745th was placed in the path of the attacking Germans when they launched their Ardennes Offensive, better known as the Battle of the Bulge. They stayed in the line until February 1945 when the German onslaught fizzled out. The battalion crossed the Rhine River in mid March and had raced through central Germany to the Czech Republic when Germany surrendered.

Norval and Burnell were coming home. Norval boarded his ship home with several hundred dollars won by gambling and selling some goods on the black market, and in his usual manner intended to pick up a couple of thousand dollars more from his fellow soldiers in crap games and playing poker.

"Well it didn't exactly happen that way," Norval recalled. "After about three days I found myself broke. I had lost every cent I had, except for the Indian Head penny I wore in a little case attached to my dog tags."

Norval had worn the Indian Head penny since coming over from the U.S.

"The strange thing was, I went down in the hole where they fed us. I was standing at a counter while I was eating and I looked down on the floor and there laid a dime." Norval chuckled aloud when he saw it.

"While I was overseas I never was paid one time. Because of my court martial and fine, they never were able to get my pay straightened out. Whenever pay day came around I never got paid. I did get 20 dollars once in Rome from the Red Cross. Any GI could walk in and get 20 bucks. I was never short of money because you could sell a pair of shoes or cigarettes or anything on the black market whenever you got into a town."

What caused Norval to chuckle was that back when he was shipped over from the U.S., he had also lost all of his money gambling, even before he boarded. On that journey over he had found a dime in his pants pocket, which gave him a total of 11 cents, counting the Indian Head penny, when he landed in North Africa.

"So the crazy thing was, I got on the ship for overseas with 11 cents and that's what I got off with when I came back."

Norval recalled that the trip home seemed long. "Everybody was anxious to get home. If I remember right, it was about eight or nine days. We were soon discharged after getting home. They sent us to a camp in Pennsylvania, what they called a separation camp, and we got our discharges there."

Norval's mom, Hazel, wrote in her special events book that Norval received his honorable discharge in September 1945, and that Burnell received his a month later.

It is remarkable that four Morey brothers served in the U.S. Army during World War II, but it is extremely impressive that three of them served in separate units that experienced some of the hottest fighting of the war on their respective fronts. It is difficult to measure how the war and Milford's death affected Norval and Burnell for the remainder of their lives. Certainly at times, particularly shortly after their return home, they would feel the world was theirs for the taking, after what they had been through and survived. But the destruction and human carnage they witnessed and contributed to left an imprint as well.

Norval's sales manager at Morbark Industries, Larry Burkholder, recalled Norval opening up to him once at a restaurant as they ate lunch. "The war did some things to him," Burkholder said. "He told me of the horrific things that he saw, the people they had to kill."

"The first time you see something, it's horrible," Norval said. "The next time it isn't so bad." Looking around the restaurant, Norval said, "If somebody jumped in here and shot four or five people, it would be a traumatic thing for you, but not for me. I could have everything cleaned up and have dinner."

Burkholder said he could see the sorrow on Norval's face when Norval talked about the kids who were lieutenants, who were sent out to lead patrols when they didn't know anything. They frequently came to Norval for advice because he had done it so much, but too often those patrols returned minus the lieutenant and or having taken too many casualties because of the lieutenant's inexperience.

"He went a year and never slept in a bed," Burkholder said. "He felt if he could just live long enough to sleep in a bed again...he talked about walking from one end of the Po Valley to the other."

Norval emphasized the importance of lawfulness, because he had seen first-hand the damage human beings were capable of inflicting on each other when law wasn't around. "You don't want to live where there's no law," he said. "If you ever saw people, what they will do...people are like animals. I've seen it."

As it did for most soldiers and for all Americans who lived during those times, the war deepened Norval's appreciation for Democracy and freedom. "You've got to be constantly aware of governments and people who will take freedom away from you," he said. "The human being is a 'funny' animal."

Norval said upon his return home his outlook on life and people could have gone either way. He could have become depressed, hardened and embittered toward everyone, and treated them roughly; or he could recognize that there was good in people and do his best to get the best out of them. He chose to follow the latter path.

"He and his brother Ralph listened to records of Roosevelt speeches and Winston Churchill speeches," Burkholder recalled. "He thought Churchill was a great man. He liked Harry Truman, thought he had guts and would say what he believed. He liked Eisenhower better than MacArthur. He didn't like MacArthur being so public relations with the pipe and everything. He felt a little bit the same about Patton."

Burkholder said Norval always had the capability to make a quick and usually accurate read of the people he came in contact with for the remainder of his life. "He could spot a phony," Burkholder said. "I think he learned a lot of that, and his beliefs and what formed him in the service."

Now back home in Winn, Norval wouldn't have much time to reflect on the tragic adventure he had just experienced and the lessons learned. The "real" world was calling.

THREE

Forquer's Tavern
Winn, Michigan
September, 1945

It seems like old times tonight at Forquer's Tavern. Three of the Morey brothers are back from the war, which is one less Morey brother than went into it. "Friendly fire" killed youngest brother Milford as he advanced into Germany only days before the end of the war. It seemed an absurd description for such a devastating event. Milford was excited to be finally getting a chance to fight Hitler. His brothers Norval, Burnell and Ralph had all begged him not to join up but he was young and wouldn't listen. Milford's body lies in the Lorraine American Cemetery near Saint-Avoid, France along with ten thousand other U.S. soldiers killed in World War II. His family intends to bring him back home soon.

Tonight, Norval, Burnell and Ralph and their sister, Lucille, are playing an on-again, off-again hand of euchre at a table cluttered with playing cards, live ashtrays, pennies and whiskey glasses. The other patrons can occasionally hear them laughing together over some inside joke and then the four of them grow silent and concentrate on their cards. The way they have the chairs tucked in around the small table lets others know that this night is for family only. Otherwise, every buddy the Morey siblings have – and there are many – will be pulling up a chair the way they usually do.

It is an especially notable evening.

In addition to grieving Milford – whom folks say, except for being shorter, was near identical to Norval in looks and mannerisms – the four Morey siblings are celebrating Norval and Burnell's return home from the war, and Norval's engagement to his girlfriend, Phyllis Barrett. Norval and Phyllis had met on his first furlough home from basic training. She had written him every other day while he was overseas and Norval had written her back whenever he could. They plan to be married in several days. The wedding will be a simple one, with the reception at the home of his future in-laws.

Burnell also has a serious girlfriend, Clara Schwartz, whom he had to leave back in Lewiston, Idaho when he joined up. He is planning to go get Clara as soon as he comes up with a sure way to support himself and a wife. Burnell and Norval have agreed to cut cedar fence posts for a fellow right outside of Winn, starting next week. They figure to make about a dollar an hour doing this but it doesn't seem like much compared to the money they'd gotten used to in the West Coast logging camps. The Army is paying each brother $20 a week unemployment and each has about $3,000 in the bank that they have saved up over the years.

The grown Morey children have been grieving, then celebrating, then grieving again for hours now. Fresh drinks come with every toast.

"Here's to Burnell," Norval says. "Welcome home to the worst faller the Northwest woods ever saw."

"Burnell," the others say while raising their glasses. Everyone takes a drink.

"Here's to, Nub," Burnell says. "Welcome home to the best fruit picker the Northwest ever saw."

"Nub," the others say, taking another drink.

"Here's to Milford," Lucille says. "My poor long lost baby brother; how bombs can be friendly, I don't know."

"Milford," they respond. Each finishes off what is left in their glass. Burnell swipes his eyes and looks over at the bartender with his index finger up to signal for another round.

When more whiskey comes, it's Norval's turn to get toasted again for the umpteenth time. Then they toast popular bride-to-be, Phyllis. Then Norval again. They play more euchre and then start over with new toasts for Burnell and Milford.

Eventually, Norval shuffles up a new hand and deals it slowly, deliberately around the table just as their father, Loyal, used to when they were kids on the farm.

It is just the four Moreys tonight. Loyal and their mother, Hazel, are in bed by now, not interested in keeping these late hours with so much work to be done in the morning. Sister Millie doesn't drink at all and baby brother, Harry, is not old enough to officially come out drinking. Eldest brother, Leo, had begged off, citing an early morning logging job to attend to. Leo has a wife and young kids at home.

The two combat veterans don't want to talk about the war. Hazel Morey has said the bad things they have seen are too fresh in their minds for her sons to talk about it just yet. But Burnell and Norval will never be comfortable talking about the war, except perhaps with each other. Lucille, now 21, doesn't push for information. She is just happy to be back among her brothers.

"Did you hear about this new thing called the G.I. Bill?" Lucille asks. "They say they will send you back to school for free if you want."

"Yeah, we heard about it," Ralph says. "Now maybe Nub can go back and finish sixth grade." Again, laughter comes from the table. Norval says, "I would have finished," Norval says, "but Mrs. Smith told me I was smarter than her, and that I might as well go home." The siblings erupt in laughter. Another round of drinks.

Norval has no thoughts of taking the government up on its offer. He's had enough heartache over the past two years to last a lifetime and has no intention of adding to it by humiliating himself in front of a roomful of fast readers, all of them children.

"I know of two things I will not do, and one of them is sitting in a stinking schoolhouse," Norval offers.

A few pennies change hands in the ensuing silence but no one is really paying any attention to the game. The liquor is having its effect. Lucille starts to sing an old hymn and they all join in.

"On a hill far away stood an old rugged cross...

"...the emblem of suffering shame; And I love that old cross where the dearest and best for a world of lost sinners was slain..."

A couple standing at the bar stares over at the table and smiles at the sight of them singing an old gospel hymn in the middle of a saloon.

"...So I'll cherish the old rugged cross till my trophies at last I lay down; I will cling to the old rugged cross, and exchange it some day for a crown."

After more quiet, more thoughts of Milford, Lucille looks over at Norval.

"Nub, tell me the other thing you ain't ever going to do, and don't start singing again."

Norval looks over at Burnell and winks. Burnell is the brother who had introduced Norval to the joys of knocking down big money.

"Yeah, Nub, what is that other thing?" Burnell asks.

Burnell didn't have Norval's restless energy or curiosity, and maybe wasn't as ambitious, but still, it was Burnell who had gone out West and found where the money was and then had shared the find with his little brother.

"Lucille, honey," Norval says. *"Here's the other thing I ain't never gonna do."* Norval's grammar, never perfect, has taken a turn for the worse after a few rounds.

"He ain't gonna wash dishes for Phyllis," Ralph says.

"We'll see about that," Burnell adds.

"What is it then?" Lucille asks.

"Brothers and sister," Norval says, rising unsteadily to his feet. Norval has his mother's dark complexion and dark, intelligent eyes. His smile is broad and engaging and his hair is combed straight back and fixed into position with Brylcreem. At age 26, he is wiry and fit as a teenager. *"As I stand here tonight, I make this solemn vow to one and all. You see my fellow Americans, I have started reading this remarkable new book."*

Laughter breaks out again at the Morey table. *"I must be in the wrong town."* Burnell says. *"You ain't never read a book in your life!"*

"Mister, what have you done with our brother Nub?" Ralph asks, laughing. *"You can't be our brother Nub if you're reading a remarkable book because our brother Nub can't read worth a damn."*

"You two shush up," Lucille says. "Let Nub say what it is he is not gonna do before I take a broom to the both of you."

"Thank you, kindly, Lucille," Norval says nodding toward his younger sister. "As I was saying, before being so rudely interrupted, I have me this book. It's by a fellow named Dale Carnegie and it's called, 'How to Win Friends and Influence People.'"

Now Norval's siblings can see he is perfectly serious. He has their complete attention.

"I'm gonna read this whole book, see? It's gonna help me NOT do the second thing I know I'm not never ever gonna do."

"My lord, Nub, what is this thing you're not doing?" Burnell asks with growing impatience.

Norval gestures with his glass to the couple still at the bar, as if to include them in his announcement, but they aren't paying attention. The book Norval is slowly struggling through has been a best seller since 1936, and sales have risen even higher as more and more veterans return home with their futures to think about.

Finally, Norval finishes his announcement.

"With help from this book I got, I ain't never gonna be poor again."

There would be a lot of "belling" going on in Winn, Michigan in the months and years immediately following the war. Norval's oldest brother, Leo, had taken the plunge back in 1934, marrying Jesse Wing. It took a while for the remaining four brothers to bite the bullet, but when they did, they did it in quick succession. Norval married Phyllis Barrett on September 8, 1945; Ralph married Ada Millard on May 13, 1946; Burnell went out to Idaho to visit his sweetheart, Clara Ann Schwartz, and they

Norval hadn't been home long, when he and Phyllis married in September 1945.

married on November 16, 1946; and Harry married Wilma Billsby on July 20, 1947.

Norval had dated Phyllis when he came home on furlough a few times prior to going overseas. "I didn't know her all that well, although she wrote very regular while I was overseas," Norval recalled. "I probably got a letter every other day. But as soon as I got home and we went out a few times, she was anxious to get married and I didn't object."

A country preacher performed the wedding for $10, with Phyllis' brother, Thurman, and Norval's sister, Lucille, standing up for the newlyweds. After the wedding they went to Forquer's tavern for a few drinks, and from there went to Phyllis' mother and stepfather's home for the reception.

"I had bought a few cases of beer and a case of whiskey and she put on the food," Norval said. There were a lot of people there and they couldn't all get in the house hardly. Those days were kind of the end of the 'belling' days, but they had to bell us, so they set off the dynamite and rung the bells and made a lot of noise."

Norval and Phyllis' wedding night was one they would never forget, but for the wrong reason. Norval consumed too much booze and as he would always be prone to do when he drank too much, he searched for the nearest bed to sleep it off in. "I didn't know where I was at," Norval said. "The first thing I knew I had crawled into bed with Phyllis' mother. She never let me live that down."

The last time Norval had gone home on furlough before going overseas, he and Phyllis had visited with Norval's grandfather, Loren Morey, who was quite ill and would pass away shortly thereafter. "Maybe some day you'll get married and live in this little house," Loren had said.

That's what happened. The house was only about 16 ft. x 18 ft., Norval recalled, with a little kitchen, a small bedroom and a living room, and some furniture. It had an oil heater and two-burner oil stove. "He had carried his water from a neighbor across the road and it had an outside john," Norval said. "But I was used to all them things. That's the way I grew up at home so it seemed natural and it was fine. I fixed the house up a little bit but I didn't have to spend very much money."

Norval never forgot his grandfather's generosity, and in later years would provide housing for several of his family members.

Norval, Phyllis, Burnell, Lucille and other family members spent much of the next few weeks in the tavern, drinking and playing cards with old buddies while doing their best not to talk about the war. Milford's absence was never far from their thoughts and the mention of him quickly caused tears to swell. The others kept telling Norval that Milford was most like him.

"After a few weeks, we decided that we had to go to work," Norval said.

They went back to doing what they knew best, felling timber, in particular felling trees that had a cedar fence post or two in them. The man they worked for paid them by the post. After working Monday through Thursday and half of a Friday, they had made $40-$45 apiece. Norval and Burnell recalled when they were each making well over $100 per week as fallers in the Northwest. "We decided right there that wasn't the thing to do," Norval said. "If the guy we were working for could make money cutting cedar and paying us, then we should go out and buy a cedar swamp."

Before Norval and Burnell had gone overseas they each put some money in the bank, and during the war they had sent some money home, some of it for their parents and the rest to be socked away. They were also now making $20 a week from the government, guaranteed for a year following their honorable discharge. "We started right then looking for a cedar swamp," Norval said. "Cedar grows pretty much in the low ground and it's good timber for fence post and, at the time, telephone poles because it would last a long time without treating in the ground."

They traveled all around the countryside on that Friday afternoon and finally on Saturday found a 40 acre cedar tract that looked promising. They ran down the owner, who said they could buy it for $1200.00, land and all. "We paid him and then went to the hardware store and bought a Swede saw, an ax, a dinner bucket and went to work," Norval said. "That would have been in late November or the first of December (1945)." A Swede saw was also known as a bow saw. It was a metal-framed saw in the shape of a bow with a coarse wide blade that was good for sawing limbs and bucking logs.

Norval didn't have a car, but Burnell had bought a used one and their dad had a car if anyone needed it. Burnell usually picked up Norval in the morning before daylight. They would drive to the tract and sit in the car and drink coffee while they waited for the light. They worked until dark. They knew the man they had been working for was getting $1 to $1.50 for poles and 30 to 40 cents for a fence post, so that's about what they charged for them.

"I think we cut somewhere in the range of 100 fence posts a day apiece plus whatever trees that were straight enough and long enough for telephone poles," Norval said. "So by the time spring came we had this 40 pretty well cut off."

Their dad joined the job then, bringing along a pair of horses to help skid the logs out of the woods. Younger brother Harry also joined up, cutting out sawlogs. "So we harvested that whole 40 without putting very much money into it," Norval said. "My father needed new buildings, so he was doing the work for the lumber for his buildings."

Burnell then left to go marry Clara in Idaho. "She was a beautiful girl with the prettiest red hair of anybody I've ever met," Norval recalled of Clara. "She wasn't only a pretty girl; she was a wonderful person."

Burnell and Clara returned to Winn so that Burnell could partner up again with Norval on their newest venture, a sawmill. Using the money they had made off the cedar tract, the Moreys purchased a used carriage and circle headsaw in Breckenridge and a used steam engine for $200 near St. Louis, Michigan. They started Morey Brothers Sawmill in 1947 on the site where a cedar mill had operated years earlier. They set up the mill on the existing concrete foundation. "I think one of them drove the engine to the mill site," recalled Larry Morey, eldest son of Leo and the first of many nephews that would work for Norval.

Fitted with manual setworks that required a block setter to stand up and ride the unit as it pushed a log into the saw and then retracted for another pass, the carriage was in disrepair and needed considerable patchwork. For one thing, its drive was worn out. Someone, perhaps John Riggle, an oldtimer the brothers sought out for advice, told them a truck rear end could be fashioned into a makeshift drive system. The Moreys probed around in local junkyards and fashioned what they needed. They also reworked the carriage log turner and made improvements to a simple board edger they had acquired. Early on they built a cutoff saw for rendering slabs into firewood—used to fire the steam engine as well as being sold to households. They later converted an old Federal one ton truck into a makeshift lift truck, stripping away most of the body, adding PTO-powered forks and turned the seat around. Although cumbersome, the rig was a reliable tool for handling logs, lumber and slabs. Riggle and Norval's brother Leo had helped Norval and Burnell in setting up the mill.

They bought their first timber tract from a man named Evart Fox and started sawing lumber. Burnell's job was to take care of the logging and getting logs to the mill, while Norval was in charge of sawing the

Norval, at left, and younger brother Harry in the sawmill.

lumber and selling it. Leo helped in the woods and Harry became involved mostly in the mill, as well. Their dad helped with both. Also their sister Lucille's husband, Andy Bardos, came on board at the mill. After working in the woods and around the mill during high school, Larry Morey went to work full time in the woods after completing high school in 1952.

They were fairly progressive and innovative for their time even though they had rather crude equipment, recalled Norval's nephew (Burnell's son), Jerry Morey. "They were the first in the state of Michigan to have a two man chain saw, an old Titan that weighed 100 pounds. They did their own logging and used Love tractors that they modified with winches. They were like the forerunner to the early skidder. They loaded the logging trucks with a block and tackle that they called a jammer."

The mill processed oak, maple, elm, ash, cherry and basswood. Logs were cut mostly into one and two inch boards, air dried on stickers for several weeks and bundled for pickup by a lumber broker with connections to the furniture factories in Reed City, 80 miles to the north-

Morey Brothers hardwood sawmill.

west. Initially lumber was sold in the rough but eventually the brothers installed a planer. Larry Morey recalled that the mill produced upward of 12,000 board feet a day, and also sold sawdust for $10 a ton to Dow Chemical Company in Midland.

Larry remembered when the sawyer would stop to do maintenance on the head saw after it hit metal or some other foreign object. "If it looked like it was going to take Shorty (the sawyer) a while to fix the saw, someone would go to the store and bring back some beer," Larry said. "We had some good times in the early days."

Larry also recalled a co-worker, Ken Moore, a woods hand who would drink with Burnell at one of the local taverns. "He and Burnell would get into it and Burnell would end up firing him. The next morning Ken would drag himself to Norval at the mill and beg for his job, and Norval would hire him back. This went on for years."

A helping hand came from a man named Harold Cook, who was an accountant in Alma that one of Norval's early lumber buyers had told Norval about. Norval had been doing the bookwork himself in pretty crude fashion. He went to see Cook, who set up a bookkeeping system for the company and continued to help Norval do the books. Cook told Norval not to worry about paying him for the work until the sawmill business had settled in. "He never cashed checks for two years until we had money," Norval said.

But money was forthcoming, and soon. "In 1947 and 1948 there hadn't been much lumber cut in the country because of the war," Norval said. "So if you had any boards that looked like lumber you could sell them at some price. It didn't take us long until we learned how to cut lumber and saw for grade, and how to dry it and sell it. It was only a few months before we were making a profit."

Norval said they made more than $10,000 after expenses in 1948, and from 1949 into the early 1950s they were making $25,000 to $35,000 a year. "So that got us started off and we were making pretty good money."

Raised on a farm near Blanchard, Larry Burkholder, who joined Norval and Morbark in 1962, remembered as a kid the growing importance of the Morey brothers in the area. Burkholder recalled when a national newspaper, *Grit*, did an article on the Morey Brothers sawmill. "That was big stuff around here," Burkholder said. "The Moreys were people you looked up to, people who had made a go of something besides farming."

Burkholder also recalled when Burnell would come to the Burkholder farm, driving a Cadillac and wearing a Stetson cowboy hat, a peculiar sight in Isabella County at the time.

Another of Burkholder's vivid childhood memories was a car crash in a pasture east of Winn in the early 1950s. Norval had visited the local bar after work and decided to set out for nearby Mount Pleasant and another watering hole. At high speed he lost control of his Lincoln Continental, left the road, plowed through a fence, rolled over several times and came to a stop upside down. Burkholder and his dad were in Winn when it happened and with many others, including Norval's wife Phyllis, rushed to the scene. Burkholder recalled, "His feet were sticking out a window and he wasn't moving. We thought he was dead." An ambulance whisked Norval to the Mount Pleasant hospital where he was treated for a broken back and fitted with a cumbersome body cast, which didn't prevent him from soon returning to the sawmill. Norval Morey would live through several other car accidents, prompting locals to say he was living a charmed life.

In 1950 the Moreys hired a man named Jim Painter to work in the woods, then later he worked in the sawmill. One of Painter's first memories of Norval was Norval sitting at his desk in the little office in the sawmill with a fifth of whiskey between his legs. "He would open it, throw the cap in the wastepaper basket and sit there, plunk, plunk, glug, glug, drink that whole fifth and you wouldn't even know he had a drink."

Norval's favorite whiskey was VO Canadian Blend. He and many of the Moreys weren't shy about hitting the booze when the time seemed right. Painter remembered Harry Morey making up some moonshine in a 50 gallon barrel drum in his basement. Painter recalled that Harry drove a vintage Star Car and one day loaded up the back with gallon jugs of moonshine and drove around Winn passing them out to his family members and friends. "Nub drank it like water," Painter said. "Then nobody could find him. He had started walking home from the mill and laid down in Bill Curtiss' back yard and went to sleep."

In addition to his drinking "skills," Norval was an excellent hunter, with the bow and rifle. "He was a damn good deer hunter and he loved to hunt rabbit," said Painter, who was no slouch himself. They went rabbit hunting with Painter's dogs almost every day they weren't working. Norval and his brother-in-law, Thurman Barrett, won the archery league more than once. For that matter Norval's wife Phyllis bagged her share of bucks as well. She wasn't afraid to hang with the boys so to speak, whether in the woods or at the area taverns.

Norval developed different relationships with each of his brothers. He never argued with Burnell, but Painter recalled Norval getting a little disgusted with the way Burnell cruised timber. "Burnell would call the number of (board) feet and I would tally the book," Painter said. "If you had like blackberry trees, they grow in clusters, three or four trees off one stump, each 6 or 8 inches, big enough to make some lumber. Burnell would add all these together and he'd call them off at 120 feet, all together. When Nub tallied the book, he thought he had a sawlog with 120 feet in it or 300 feet or whatever it was; instead he had maybe five little ones and they weren't half as valuable. Nub used to get on me and he said when Burnell calls them like that don't mark them in the book like that. But I'd mark them just like Burnell told me to."

Harry was good with equipment and good around the mill and good at keeping everybody on their toes. He would drive his vintage Star full speed onto the mill yard in the morning and try to scale the heights of the sawdust pile, splattering dust, mud and snow, only to come to a stop, shudder and roll back down, nearly turning over. Harry and Norval's relationship would gradually deteriorate through the years. Leo was only five years older than Norval, but always seemed a lot older, one reason being that by 1950 he had already been married for 15 years. Two of his children were born even before the War. Ralph wasn't

Norval with Connie next to air-dried lumber; Norval's mom, Hazel, and grandchild Connie; the young family, Phyllis and Norval with baby Lon, Connie and Betty.

involved in the sawmill. He ran a butcher shop in Midland, but would join the family business soon enough.

As the hardwood lumber business established itself, Norval and Phyllis figured it was time to establish a family. In fact the Morey siblings during the next few years added significantly to the population of Isabella County. Norval and Phyllis had two daughters, Connie and Betty, born in 1946 and 1948, and then a son, Lonnie, born in 1950. Ralph's son, Mike, was born in 1946. Burnell's son, Jerry, was born in 1947, the first of seven children (Linda, Ilene, Sharon, John, Tom and William). Lucille's first child, James, was born in 1948, followed by Ronald, Gary and Debra over the next several years. Harry's first child, Milford, was born in 1949, followed by Joyce, Edward and June. Sister Mildred's first child, Jonathan, was born in 1951, followed by Susan (who died shortly after birth) and Melanie. Leo's third child, Myron, was born in 1947, following Shirley and Larry, the two eldest cousins of this impressive clan.

In the midst of all of these baby announcements, the Moreys, like many families throughout the country, were still dealing with the tragic ramifications of the War. Milford's body, which had been buried in the Lorraine American Cemetery near Saint Avold, France, was returned home on February 3, 1949 and buried with military funeral rites at Union Cemetery, following a service at his parents' home. Then on May 30, 1952, Winn Park was dedicated in Milford's honor, and a large stone monument with Milford Morey's name was placed there.

Another loss hit Norval and the Morey family, when Norval's

A special ceremony and monument in Winn recognized Milford Morey's supreme sacrifice.

dad Loyal died suddenly at the farm home on February 7, 1956. He had been a tremendous help to Morey Brothers Lumber, which the obituary referred to as "one of Winn's most thriving industries." The obituary stated of Loyal: "In his life in this area he had earned the respect of all who knew him." Loyal was 62 years old. He left behind his wife, Hazel, but he certainly didn't leave her alone, as most of the children remained in the area along with an impressive roster of grandchildren. Loyal had built another home some years before, where he and Hazel had been living more comfortably after moving from the original homestead cabin. Norval and Phyllis as well had built a home up the hill from the sawmill and across the street, moving out of the close confines of Norval's grandfather's old house.

Had Loyal lived, he would certainly have enjoyed and participated in Norval's newest business venture, which began by happenstance the year after Loyal's death; a venture that would ultimately change everything for Norval and the Morey family, for the people who lived in and around Winn, for the entire forest products industry in the United States and for the wood-to-energy movement that surfaced in the 1970s and which was re-born in the first decade of the 21st century.

It didn't begin with such visions of grandeur, but it did begin with a vision of sorts.

A heavy drinking machinist named Bob Baker said he was laying on a river bank during a trout fishing outing, watching some loggers standing over an open fire heating up their draw shaves and spuds for peeling bark off frozen pulpwood logs. As Baker observed this scene he said his head started spinning (or perhaps continued to spin) and the vision of a machine that turned the log over a cutting device to remove the bark came to him. Removing bark from logs was a prerequisite to manufacturing paper, and pulp and paper companies were operating very cost-intensive, and mostly inefficient machinery at their mills for removing the bark. But no machinery device for this task existed for in-woods operations. Baker approached the owner of Benedict's Machine Shop in Big Rapids, where Baker had worked before, and the owner allowed Baker access to some tools and workspace in the upstairs portion of the shop. Baker went to work on building a model of the contraption and soon had built a working portable version, which he called a pulpwood peeler. Baker started looking into how to go about gaining a patent for it and getting the word out about it. He eventually landed in the law office of a lawyer in Big Rapids named Frank Ryman.

It so happened that Ryman was the same man who many years ago had hired Norval Morey to cut and trim trees on new rights-of-way for the Rural Electrical Association. Ryman, who was from Ohio, had married a girl from Winn, Coreen Himebaugh, before the War, and then after he got out of the Army they settled in Winn, where Ryman did odd jobs while she ran the post office. Ryman decided to go to law school, passed the bar and eventually established his law office in Big Rapids, which was where Bob Baker found him.

Norval and Ryman had stayed in touch through the years and Norval frequently visited Ryman in Big Rapids. Usually Norval stopped by after going to Reed City, where Norval regularly called on a lumber buyer. "I would stop back in Big Rapids at Frank's office and would shoot the bull with him for an hour or two on my way home," Norval said. One day as Norval was leaving Ryman's office, Ryman casually said, "If a guy had a little money, there are lots of good deals that go through the law office." To which Norval responded, "Well, I have a little money and if the right deal comes along, let me know."

A few weeks later Ryman called Norval. "You know there was a crazy guy in here yesterday," Ryman said. "I don't presume he's got anything that amounts to much, but it might be something you ought to take a look at. He says he's invented a pulpwood peeler. I told him about you and that you might be interested in it. If you are, why come on over."

Norval went to Ryman's office in Big Rapids, then Ryman called Bob Baker into his office. "He was drunk," Norval said. "He explained the debarker he had built and what a great thing it was. Eventually he took me to see it. What it was, was sort of a working model of his idea. He had a bunch of small poplar poles probably two or three inches in diameter and about three feet long. He could spin them right through there and take the bark off. It was a fascinating thing.

"I didn't know anything about a debarker and I had no idea what the market was or if there was even a market," Norval said.

Baker explained that the current modus operandi in the woods was scraping off the bark with a hand tool. The more Norval looked into, the greater the potential he saw. Certainly the removal of bark by hand was antiquated, and paper mills were currently wrestling with how to mechanically remove bark from logs at their mill sites, either by soaking and softening the logs and then removing the bark with water pressure, or bouncing the logs around in a rotating drum until the bark fell away. But these methods were costly and what paper mills really desired was a cost-efficient machine that could process several cords of wood per hour at locations removed from the mill, either in the forest or at remote log storage wood yards. Some machines had been proposed that scraped off the bark, but they didn't work well on frozen logs in the winter, which was the best time to be transporting timber out of the woods to the mill.

"It soon became obvious to me that if you built a machine big enough and it operated right, there would be a market for it," Norval said.

Norval struck up a deal with Baker. Norval would pay Baker several hundred dollars up front, as Baker needed some money right away to make up some back payments on his car. Norval would find a patent attorney and apply for a patent with both of their names on it. Meanwhile, Norval would pay wages to Baker and to one of Baker's machinist buddies, Sid Hay, as they started building the machine, and Norval would finance the materials and also cut a deal with Benedict's Machine Shop to build the machine there and for use of the shop machinery.

"My biggest problem was keeping them working," Norval recalled. "When Bob had money, he was drinking. He didn't put in too many hours a week."

With Norval's constant prodding, they pieced together a prototype machine, ran some logs through it and it seemed to do okay. Norval thought it would be a good idea to develop some blueprints and cutting order prints to be able to take to a manufacturer for building the machine. He found an engineering firm in Grand Rapids and paid them $4,000 for drawing up the prints. "At that time, that was a lot of money," Norval said.

Once he obtained the prints he contacted Henry Brettrager, who owned a fabrication shop in Saginaw. Ed Brettrager was Henry's younger brother and worked for Henry at the shop. "When Morey first came in he was driving a Volkswagon Beetle and pulling a machine," Ed recalled. "He said he had asked the patent attorney who could help build these machines up, and the attorney said go see Henry Brettrager. We built one and he took it out and used it a few days and it fell apart. It wasn't heavy enough. Then he come back and we beefed it up in different places so it would stand up. It come back a couple of times and we had some adjusting to do. Then they started selling them just as fast as we built them."

It didn't happen quite so quickly. When Norval went to see Henry for the first time, prints in hand, they agreed that Brettrager would build a dozen of them for around $2,500 each.

"It appeared to me that if we could sell it for $3,000 or $3,500 we could make some money," Norval said. "So Brettrager cut up material for seven or eight machines and proceeded to start manufacturing them."

After several weeks in late 1957, Brettrager completed a machine and had two more nearly finished with gasoline Wisconsin engines. "We had put some beveled gears on it to drive the feed wheels, which were different and had really not been tested," Norval said. They took the debarker to a sprawling wood yard in Clare owned by Watervliet Paper Company, about 20 miles from Winn. "We ran the machine a day or two and they could see it was going to be a money maker for them to peel this pile of wood out. They had about 10,000 cords of wood there. They had a couple of people (contractors) that wanted to buy a machine. So we sold them the first machine for $3,500 and I believe they ordered a second machine that we would be delivering a few days later."

But after only a few days of operation, the gears went out because of bark buildup. Norval and Brettrager put in new gears and tried again. After a couple of more days, the gears went out. "So it was quite obvious that the gears weren't the way to go," Norval said. "That ruined the whole machine. It was designed around that and it would have to be completely changed in order to work."

Following the problem with the gears, Norval told Brettrager, who had several thousand dollars in fabrication material on the shop floor, to cease production. Meanwhile Norval purchased the Hutchins' blacksmith's shop in downtown Winn. The shop

Norval working on the first portable debarker.

came with a forge, drill press, a welder and few other tools. Norval, Harry and Don Strong, who had begun work at Morey Brothers Sawmill in 1956, took one of the machines to the blacksmith's shop and started making changes.

Many years after his death, one of the items found in Norval's

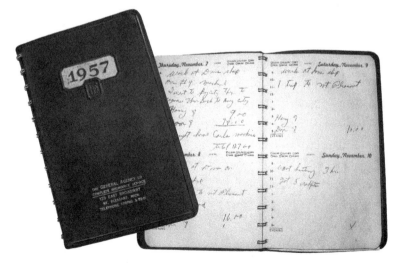

Norval kept daily notes on the development of the portable peeler in a 1957 daily planner.

belongings at Morbark was a 1957 daily planner book. Norval had written very little in it until October, when his notes and comments are fully focused on the development of the pulpwood peeler. His diary shows almost daily travels to various machine shops, to nearby timber tracts to try out the machine, to the Clare wood yard, and to visit his lawyer. He also listed the first names of people and the hours that they had worked for him each day on the project.

Here's a sampling of some of Norval's entires exactly as he entered them:

October 10: Harry and I work on peeler at mill, took one top yoke off and try it, worked good, took peeler out to Paris 3 times.

October 11: Harry and I worked on peeler at mill, took off 1 bottom yoke, took out to Paris 2 times to try machine, work good.

October 15: Harry and I went out to peel wood on Paris in fournoon, try out peged wheel on back yolk.

October 28: try out machine with chain drive. It works fair. Still needs some changes.

October 29: went to Clare, peeled wood. Made about 4 cords per hr.

October 30: I went to Saginaw, picked up new machine with chain drive. Back to Winn, then to Clare. Harry and Don peeled all day there.

October 31: Tried out machine. Brettrager built chain drive. Did not work at all.

November 1: Changed machine #3. The wheels on top to steel wheels. They didn't work too good.

November 2: Seen Don Urie about shop to work in.

November 4: Started at Don shop on new machine #4.

November 8: Worked at Don's on #4 machine. 2 trips to Mt. Pleasant. 1 to Alma.

November 10: Went hunting. Got 5 rabbits.

November 15, 16, 17: Hunting.

November 19: Worked on Carl's machine. I went to Mt. Pleasant, picked up 2 10" wheels & pegs.

November 23: Work on Carl's machine. Try it out, is going to work good.

November 25: Went to Clare, try out Carl's machine with chain drive. Need some more work on it.

November 26: Bob and I went to Bay City. Harry and Don and Sid work on machine.

November 27: Took machine up to Leo in fornoon, try on green wood, took it to Clare in afternoon. Worked out good.

December 2: Started new machine with verabele speed pulley, went to Saginaw, got back late at night.

December 19: took machine to Saginaw for Brettrager to start building. Don Strong went with me. We went to Clare on way back.

December 22: Had Xmas dinner at hall in Winn. Family was all there.

December 26: Carl broke shaft in machine at Clare.

As noted, considerable work was also done at a welding shop in Mount Pleasant with Don Urie, who was married to Norval's aunt. The men continued to work on the machine into the new year and made great strides. "We laid out a chain driven machine where the feed wheels would have a chain drive and used scrap stuff to build it up with," Norval said. "My brother Leo had 40 acres of aspen wood just north of Winn and every time we got it to where we thought it would work we took it up there and ran a little wood through it. Then we'd come back and do more work on it. After a few weeks we had a machine that we could slam a lot of wood through."

Jim Painter also assisted Norval, Harry and Strong in the blacksmith's shop. Painter recalled that Strong's input was crucial to the final, successful development of the pulpwood peeler, in particular how the feed rolls spiraled the wood through the machine. "Things went a lot better after he got in there," Painter said of Strong.

It wasn't until 1959 that the United States Patent Office issued patent number 2,912,023 for a Log Debarking Apparatus, assigned to Robert M. Baker and Norval K. Morey. Unique to the invention was the "floating cutterhead," which became the Morbark "debarking principle." It featured a cutterhead affixed with carbide tipped teeth and locked on a floating table beneath the log. The log was advanced and

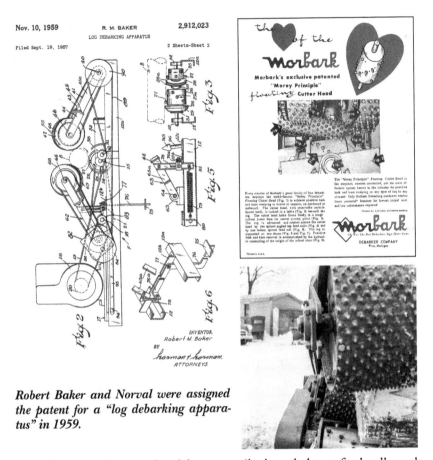

Robert Baker and Norval were assigned the patent for a "log debarking apparatus" in 1959.

rotated across the cutterhead by two spiked angled top feed rolls and one bottom spiked feed roll. In essence the machine conformed to the contour of the log to gain maximum bark removal. Initially the machine was suitable for logs from three to 16 inches in diameter and up to 20 feet long. It weighed approximately 2,500 pounds and was about 12 feet long, seven feet wide and six feet high. It required two to three men to operate the trailer-mounted machine.

While the development of the pulpwood peeler was ongoing in late 1957, and needing a company name for his bookkeeping, Norval came up with Morbark Portable Debarker Company, borrowing from Norval's last name and obviously the term "bark." Norval considered "Morbake" in recognition of Bob Baker, but felt "bark" was kind of close to Baker's name and obviously "Morbark" revealed the purpose of the new machine.

Once the machine seemed right, Norval and his companions took it back to Watervliet's wood yard at Clare, where the company still had 10,000 cords awaiting to be debarked. Watervliet had installed a Cambio ring debarker, more often seen in sawmills, to run the wood through, but the wood had sat there too long and that kind of debarker tore up the logs. Norval figured the company had paid $10 to $12 a cord for the wood, so he was sure they would pay $3 or $4 a cord to get it peeled. Indeed they offered $3.50 a cord, and Harry and Don Strong set up the machine and in the first day peeled more than $350 worth of wood. The wood yard manager anxiously called Norval and said he needed to come up to the yard. When Norval arrived the manager stated frankly there was no way the company could afford to pay that kind of money for peeling the wood. Norval offered to peel it for a dollar less a cord, but the manager wouldn't go for it. Norval said they would just have to buy a machine, and they actually bought two, put them in the wood yard and over the next six months they debarked all of the wood.

But Norval and the fledgling company was in dire financial straits. Norval had spent a lot of money on the development and fabrication of the machine, including almost of $30,000 he had borrowed from the bank, which loaned him the money because of his sawmill business. Norval had hesitated to mention what he really needed the money for. "We were at the stage where we had to sell some machines or be in trouble," Norval said.

Norval took the machine for a demonstration at S. D. Warren's wood yard at Muskegan, Michigan. They peeled wood for a week and S. D. Warren wrote Norval a check for $20,000 for five machines. "If it hadn't been for that sale, very possibly we would have never got started," Norval said. Norval paid most of the money to Henry Brettrager for the money Brettrager had put into the machines.

Norval and his workers continued to demonstrate the machine and sell them one at a time, and the venture seemed to be gaining momentum. Norval found a dealer in the Upper Peninsula who thought he could sell a hundred machines but Norval was concerned that Brettrager could-

The Morbark debarker could handle big ones as well as little ones.

$3450.⁰⁰

F. O. B. Winn, Mich.
Base Price
Model P-420A
Illustrated Above

POWER UNITS AVAILABLE
Prices Installed on Debarker)

WISCONSIN Model T642 ... $750⁰⁰
... with gentle grip 57 HP
PWISONTAL Model S766 ... $1095⁰⁰
one wind pipeline press 28M
CONTINENTAL Model S2200 ... $1655⁰⁰
... for a sore wind 78.5, Min. 38.4

MORBARK
PORTABLE DEBARKER CO.
Winn, Michigan
"THE WAY THE BEST DEBARKERS SIGN THEIR NAME"

n't build them fast enough. Norval had Don Strong contact Benedict's in Big Rapids and they made a deal to build machines. "They built 25 machines there and Brettrager built about 25 machines in Saginaw. The problem was they didn't sell as fast as we thought and I was back in financial trouble again." Norval and Harry continued to demonstrate the machine and sell them a few at a time to various companies such as S. D. Warren, Packaging Corporation and Consolidated Paper in Wisconsin. Finally Norval scored big time with Nekoosa-Edwards Paper also in Wisconsin, which purchased 50 machines in one order, with Morbark to deliver two machines per week until the order was filled. "These sales are what really got Morbark started," Norval recalled.

The young company gained some free publicity when American Pulpwood Association reported in a technical release that maintenance on the machine was proving to be very low, and that one set of carbide-tipped cutters peeled more than 1,000 cords without sharpening. Meanwhile word was rapidly spreading that when pulpwood, especially aspen, was debarked prior to shipping, substantial savings accrued in transportation and handling.

"We had a small crew of all hard working people and we had very little overhead," Norval said. "Whenever we sold a machine we could pay for the material and have some left to build another one."

Desiring more control over the accelerated fabrication of his machine and the costs therein, Norval in 1958 decided to build his own shop behind his home on Winn Road, up the hill from the sawmill. He had been using the basement in his house as an office, assisted by his secretary, Lucy Curtiss. Tucked inside the 1957 day book found at Morbark was Norval's original, very rough pencil sketching for a 64 foot by 80 foot shop along with an inventory and costs of the lumber, plywood, steel posts, concrete and other raw materials, plus labor costs for construction of the building. His brother-in-law, Thurman Barrett, oversaw the project, which cost the company $7,500. Through the years, that original 5,000 square feet would expand into a 1.6 million square feet manufacturing complex.

Somewhere around this period Norval apparently sold his share of the sawmill business to Burnell, according to Burnell's son, Jerry, and used the money to further establish Morbark. Norval also pulled some employees from the sawmill over to Morbark. Sales of the portable debarker escalated to the point that by mid 1959 at least two dozen companies were using one or more of the machines, including a few companies in the Southern U.S. Norval and Morbark expanded the debarker line to peel longer and bigger logs, suitable for smaller stationary sawmills as well as for portable setups. Morbark also offered the live decks, conveyors and other feeding accessories to go with them. Norval and Strong mounted a unit on a trailer and took it down to New Orleans for display at the Southern Pine Exposition and returned with two orders from an operation in North Carolina. One of Norval's biggest supporters in the South, who always seemed to be there when Norval's business was on the wane in the early years, was Johnson-Sherman Company of Goldsboro, NC, which would order batches of machines and pay for them in advance, in effect loaning Morbark operating capital. Business slowed considerably at a point in 1960 and Norval couldn't make payroll. Norval's son, Lon, recalled, "Morbark is in existence today because of Robert Johnson. Robert ordered 30 debarkers and paid him cash up front. Dad never forgot. They were one of our best dealers, too." Norval made sure nobody at Morbark ever forgot either.

Norval's brother Ralph joined the company as sales manager and proved to be an effective promoter, especially in the South and Northeast as Morbark rounded up dealerships to represent the debarker line. Morbark's timing and success with the log debarker was synonomous with the expanding paper industry and its growing acceptance of chips. An article appearing in a 1961 issue of *Southern Lumberman* noted that in 1960 there were about 900 log processing plants in the South, primarily sawmills, making and selling chips to paper mills. Log slabs and edgings had heretofore had scant value, but once sawmill owners realized these pieces could be processed into chips for paper mills, many invested in debarkers to prepare the log for finer sawing, and its off pieces more suitable for the production of cleaner chips.

Jim Painter recalled a couple of debarker episodes from the early years. "We built several types of debarkers in them days," Painter said. "Harry built one model that was called the Flattop. Bill Richardson and Nub and I went up to Kimberly-Clark Corporation at Sunrise Landing, in the UP. We took an Airstream trailer up there and worked seven days. It was colder than hell. Nub done the cooking; Bill and I run the machine. We hired a guy with a front-end loader to bring the wood to the machine and take it away. Nub would make up a nice big hot toddy and bring it to us from time to time. He would take over and relieve one of us, giving Bill and me a chance to get warm."

Another memorable event took place at North Bay, Ontario at the mill wood yard of Watervliet Paper Company. As Painter tells it: "One day not long after Nub had bought a new Mercury station wagon, he said to me, 'Get your clothes together, we're going for a ride.' We went to North Bay to repair a W4 debarker. It was bitter cold. The machine was at the mill wood yard, which was deserted. We found the problem and towed the debarker to a machine shop to get some blocks made to repair it, then towed it to back to the wood yard to try it out. It was so damn cold. Nub was running the machine and I was putting the wood on—big popple. Not one soul came out there to help us. Finally, the woodlands manager came out wearing a big Eskimo type coat. Nub said to him, 'It seems like with all your people we could have a little bit of help out here.' The man replied, 'When it's 35 below zero we shut the wood yard down.' So Nub shut the debarker down right then. We threw our stuff in the car and headed for Michigan. We'd only got about two miles down the road when the car radiator froze up. We put some old coats over the radiator to warm 'er up and got 'er going again and took off for home."

Debarker sales of all types escalated after Norval hired Hank Shepherd, who had previously worked as a forest engineer for the American Pulpwood Association and before that worked for Bob Larson, developer of one of the forest industry's first knuckleboom loaders. Shepherd saw potential in the small debarker and approached Norval about joining the team. "Eventually I hired him and he introduced us around the country to a lot of different paper mills and that was another help in getting us started in the industry," Norval said. Norval also remembered that Shepherd "introduced the people that worked for me to how to spend money, stay in good hotels and eat in expensive restaurants, which I wasn't used to and wasn't in favor of." Shepherd also led Morbark to industry meetings and trade shows, and though Norval had doubts at the time about the expense involved, he later acknowledged that "it did us more good than what I thought at the time for the cost of it."

Larry Morey tells of a big multi-machine order that Shepherd secured soon after he joined Morbark and the spirit of celebration surrounding it. Morbark employed only about 10 at the time and Christmas Day was drawing near. Norval responded by throwing a party, giving each worker a turkey, a pay increase and a new wallet with a crisp $100 bill tucked inside.

That gesture set the tone for Norval's enduring employee outreach that went on for decades. He loved to mingle with the workers on the floor during the day, assessing their attitude and observing their effort, diligence and performance. He took it deeper, often joining them after hours at the workplace to have a drink and shoot the breeze. Not one to take himself too seriously, Norval had a good sense of humor and enjoyed a good joke, although he was not regarded as a gifted joke teller. He sought workers who showed up on time, were consistent, gave it their all and took pride in their craft. He found an ample supply of such labor in Isabella and surrounding counties.

Norval wanted such commitment from his dealership partners as well. Several independent dealers, in addition to Johnson-Sherman Company in North Carolina, helped to support Morbark in the early years. Other notable dealers included Ned Johnson Machinery Company, Winnfield, La.; A.L. Bogg Machinery Co., Jefferson City, Mo.; Hawkensen Enterprises, Plymouth, NH; Lyons Sawmill & Logging Equipment & Supply, Little Valley, NY; Armstrong Equipment, Birmingham, Ala.; Teets Equipment Company, Terra Alta, W. Va.

Jack Haygood, son of a sawmiller and a former pulpwood producer, began selling Morbark debarkers for a dealer in Georgia in 1961. He had no sales experience but was a hard worker, understood the sawmill community and was mechanically inclined. Haygood not only sold his share but also came up with a simple solution to keep the debarker from throwing belts. Norval flew to Atlanta to see for himself the bracket Haygood had come up with, made a rough drawing of it and returned to Michigan. The bracket became a standard item on the machine. Norval and Haygood developed a close relationship. When Norval formed Morbark of Georgia, a company-owned store, Haygood joined the organization and took his sales performance to a higher level. Haygood recalled that Norval took note of this and surprised him at a Christmas party in Winn, presenting him with a $10,000 bonus. "He said I'd sold a good percentage of all debarkers made that year and that he wanted to reward me," Haygood said. "I was happy to get the recognition and the money."

Norval said that during the early '60s Morbork sold from two to three million dollars worth of equipment each year, increasing to the four to five million dollar range by the middle of the decade, and would usually make at least ten percent profit. "So we're adding on to the manufacturing facility practically every year and buying used and new equipment to do a better job of manufacturing," he said.

The sawmill business meanwhile wasn't faring as well. Norval was totally focused on Morbark, leaving Burnell at the helm of the lumber business and perhaps with lesser quality workers as some of them moved to the Morbark plant with Norval. (Norval had set up another company for the actual plant operations called Morey Manufacturing, of which Norval's brother Leo was now the plant foreman.) Burnell's son, Jerry, recalled that the lumber market went into the tank. And at the same time Burnell continued to have a drinking problem, according to Jerry, which was enhanced by the problems at the sawmill, but which also probably stemmed from his horrific war experiences. The war may also have contributed to Norval's heavy drinking much of his life, especially during the early years of Morbark when Norval might consume a fifth of whiskey during the day. When the sawmill business wound down, Burnell worked at the Morbark plant, sometimes on one of the fabrication lines or representing one of the debarker products.

Norval spoke highly of Burnell and his wife Clara as wonderful parents of seven children. "Burnell was a very good father and was very proud of those kids," Norval said. "He bought a cabin at Diamond Lake and they spent all their summers up there and the kids had to have a lot of fun growing up. But my brother Burnell had a problem. After we'd made quite a little money, he got to not working too hard and drinking too much. That happens to a lot of people. He had a hard time overcoming that. But what was important is he did take good care of his family and they all grew up to be wonderful people."

Norval and Phyllis' three children, Connie, Betty and Lon, had become young teenagers or close to it, each separated by about two years in age. They, too, spent much of their summers on the water at a small cabin on the Muskegon River, with Norval driving over on Friday night or Saturday after work. Phyllis' brother, Thurman, who had helped Norval build the cabin, and Thurman's wife, Marge, spent a lot of time there. Plenty of other company visited as well. A card game was always going on. "It didn't matter how many came to the river on the weekend, different people that worked for me and other friends, Phyllis always found something to eat for everybody and never complained. Phyllis was never afraid of hard work," Norval said, adding that the same held true when the Moreys entertained business visitors at their home in town.

"It was a good place for the kids to swim and travel on the river in the summer, and it was a great place for hunting in the fall during deer season. We had a lot of fun there when the kids were growing up," Norval said.

Norval also fondly recalled a fiberglass flat bottom boat Thurman had built. "We used to cruise up and down the river for miles and miles both ways."

His daughter Betty said some of her most pleasant memories were her experiences at the river. "That was our life, at the river, our cottage. We did a lot of boating, berry picking. He taught us how to respect the river and still have fun with it. He taught us how to swim in the river."

Betty recalled their experiences tubing down the river with her dad and her grandma (Phyllis' mom). "It was a long day," she said. "That was big for him."

Betty recalled when tornadoes were in the area and her dad went outside and dug a hole big enough for Norval, Phyllis and their three children to fit in. The hole remained with a covering on it for possible future use. The last time Norval had dug such a hole, the sound of thunder had also swept through the air, only then it was incoming German artillery.

Betty also admired her mom's ability to manage crowds of visitors, and that such hospitality was always part of her mom's nature. "My mom did so much for people," Betty said. "She did so much for Winn.

When there was a need she was there to help. When people died, she was there."

Younger brother Lon agreed that their mother would do anything for anyone in trouble. When Lon's uncle Burnell and aunt Clara lost a 19-year-old daughter, Linda, to hepatitis in 1968, Phyllis and Connie, who was a few years older than Linda, watched over the other children and took clothing to Clara who stayed at the hospital.

Like his sisters, Lon enjoyed the river as well, and was always amazed at the amount of alcohol that his dad consumed, whether it was while boating down the river or playing cards. "He could drink more than any man I had ever seen and not get really drunk," Lon said. "But he could get real drunk, too."

Lon began working for his father's company when he was eight years old, helping Thurman to put in the foundation of the first factory in the Morey's backyard. "Thurman probably chewed me out, but I was supposedly helping him lay the blocks for the first foundation," Lon said. Lon recalled he became a regular on the payroll at about age 12.

Except for some college, Lon never left his dad's business, but their relationship was strained, Lon said, from the beginning. "I knew at a very young age he was an influential person in the community and being the son of somebody like that has more downfalls than advantages. He was not per se a father. I can only recall him playing catch with me once. We didn't see eye to eye but we didn't verbally argue about things all the time. It probably made me a more responsible person later on."

The first time Lon "got drunk" was with his father while the Morbark Christmas party, at home, was winding down. Lon, who was 15, came home to find his father, his uncle Burnell and some others from the company well intoxicated. Lon proceeded to drink an entire bottle of champagne, followed by some serious intake of a fifth of VO Canadian Blend, Norval's favorite, and then sat down with the men and argued religion. Lon finally passed out on the floor and had the dry heaves for two days. "I can say I got drunk with my father the first time I ever got drunk," Lon said.

Norval's first inquiry of Lon as to his interest in Morbark came when Lon was 17 and living with his cousin Jim Bardos in a trailer that an employee had given over to Norval. Their exchange was brief and blunt. Lon recalled: "He was having some medical problems and the doctors were telling him he had hardening of the arteries, and a lot of what they were saying wasn't right. He came out to the trailer and came right out and asked me what my interest was in the company. I told him 'if it's going to make me into what you are, I don't want anything to do with it. But yes I am interested in the company.' What I was talking about was he wasn't a father to me or a good family man, like I wanted to be."

Lon tried college twice, first in Worchester, Massachusetts and then nearer to home at Central Michigan University, but it didn't agree with him, and he returned full time to Morbark.

Lon's sister, Betty, however, thought Norval was a good father, always there for her. "He was a whiz in math," she said. "If there was a problem I had, he didn't do it the way they did it, but he always came up with the answer. He may not have been with us for the quantity of time, but he took care of us kids. Him and Lon never had the relationship they both wanted, but they were both stubborn."

In the twilight of his life, Norval had some regrets about his fatherhood, but fully praised Phyllis for her role. "Phyllis was a great mother to the kids," he said. "She took good care of them. They were always dressed well and clean. I'm sure I didn't pay much attention. In those days I was working six or seven days a week in the mill. I had 18 or 20 people working for me. So I neglected my family from that standpoint."

Norval said his lack of education growing up contributed to another weakness as a father. "I think we both neglected them when it came to their education, and things like that were probably more important than either one of us realized. I always thought, like a lot of other people, that you send them to school and the teacher will take care of it. My mother and father when it came to that couldn't help me much, and I thought 'well I got by all right, they will, too.' But that was not the way it should have been. We didn't encourage them enough to get a good education and I don't think we let them go ahead and do things they should have been doing."

Norval's education had ended early in the seventh grade and a difficulty with reading, and comprehending what he had read remained with him. This forced him to read slowly and to read the same thing over and over again until he got it. Often he had people at work read promotion materials to him. But once he understood, he had an excellent ability to remember it.

An early favorite book of Norval's was Dale Carnegie's "How to Win Friends and Influence People." He once said to his brother Ralph "I'm not going to be poor, I'm going to have money," and Ralph asked him how he was going to do it. Norval said, "I don't know but I got this book." Norval brought in consultants from Dale Carnegie to teach courses to Morbark personnel on self-improvement and salesmanship. Lon Morey was 16 when he took the course at Morbark as instructed by Michael Handley from Saginaw, Michigan. Ironically, after Norval died and Lon assumed sole leadership of Morbark, Lon brought in Michael Handley's son, Dan, of Handley & Associates to teach Dale Carnegie principles to Morbark managers. Father and son, in different eras, used the same methods to pull Morbark employees in the same direction.

Meanwhile the business of Morbark took greater shape. In 1964 Norval partnered with Bob McBain, the owner of the accounting firm retained by Morbark, to purchase the old American Logging Tool Corporation in Evart, Michigan. The company manufactured common logging tools such as cant hooks, pike poles, wedges and tongs. The company was unionized at the time and Norval dismissed all of the management personnel and put the plant manager in charge, telling him he'd shut the plant down if the union remained intact. It didn't. The company was a good investment but its products eventually ran their course with the encroachment of logging mechanization.

While Morbark continued to expand its line of debarkers, Norval refused to manufacture a rosserhead type debarker, such as that manufactured by a competitor. Norval considered the rosserhead method inferior to the Morbark principle. Some 30 years later, when Norval's health was in decline, some underlings at the company led the development of a rosserhead debarker and the plant began building them. Larry Burkholder was at the plant when Norval discovered one on the factory floor. "He came in one day and spotted the machine. 'What the hell's that?' I said it was a rosserhead debarker. 'Geez, when did we come out with that?' I told him it had been almost a year ago. 'Hmmm, I wonder who they think is running this place? I've spent the better part of my life fighting against that thing and I sure as hell ain't going to change and build it now.'" Production was halted immediately, and Morbark didn't resume rosserhead debarker production until the late 1990s, after Norval's death.

Burkholder had joined Morbark in 1962 as kind of a combination bookkeeper and sales assistant to Norval's brother, Ralph. Burkholder, who had grown up on a nearby farm, was pursuing accounting as a profession with a plan to become a state bank examiner. He studied at American Business Institute, worked as a loan officer at Blanchard State Bank, and started specializing in income tax work. He hired out

Morbark expanded its debarker line.

for some part-time work for a local lumber company doing their bookkeeping and taxes. Norval stopped by the operation one day and stuck his head in when Larry was there, and told Larry he was looking for a bookkeeper. Larry informed Norval that he was accumulating a lot of background in accounting though he didn't have a specialized degree. "Norval was at ease with people who didn't think they were experts," Burkholder recalled. A few days into his job at Morbark, Burkholder was given access to the company's loose financial records, piled in a basket, and told to go through them and assess Morbark's financial condition. "I don't think I could go broke in less than a year, do you?" Norval asked. Burkholder said the books were a mess. "I didn't realize what I'd gotten myself into." After deciphering the data, Burkholder suggested that Norval should cut the employee count and trim other expenses, which Norval proceeded to do.

Not on the employee roster in those early years was a trained engineer. "Nub had a minimum high regard for engineers," Burkholder said. "If you mentioned the word engineer he'd go ballistic."

Several years before his death, Norval was asked about his engineering background. He grimaced, then slightly smiled and replied, "Me? I can't even spell engineering." Thinking back on his upbringing, he added, "It's not something that takes a genius. It's just something you grow up with."

In the mid 1960s Norval brought back the mothballed sawmill, partly as a demonstration mill for Morbark products. Norval's brother, Harry, managed the sawmill. The mill operated a Bush 48 inch chipper, and Norval felt it was over-engineered, which prompted him to begin toying around with chipper designs in his head. Norval struck up a deal to sell Bush chippers, but the arrangement was short-lived. According to Norval, when several Bush employees left that company to form their own to supply chipper parts, Norval and Morbark helped to fund the company's effort to become a chipper manufacturer and more specifically to build a Morbark chipper, which is how it went for a while. But that relationship ended when Norval felt some shenanigans were going on involving the chipper manufacturer's direct sales of Morbark chippers, gaining the company another 10 to 20 percent over what Morbark was paying to buy the chippers from the company.

Norval said one of the chipper manufacturer's partners had informed him of the direct sales, and Norval promptly hired him and another man with chipper manufacturing experience to start up Morbark's new chipper manufacturing operation, and turned the project over to Don Strong, one of Norval's right-hand men who had been so instrumental in the development of the Morbark peeler. "Don went down to Alabama where most chipper parts were made and made deals with different companies to get the materials. It didn't take us very long until we were in the chipper business," Norval recalled. "Of course we were way behind our dealers and customers. We had probably 50 orders for chippers that we weren't able to fill and they were waiting for a new Morbark chipper to come out. We were very lucky with the first chipper we built. It worked fine and the customers soon caught on and bought a lot of chippers from Morbark."

During the ensuing years, chipping machinery became Morbark's bread and butter. Norval's nephew, Jerry, who had started working for the company as a young teenager, recalled that Norval had good business insight and could assess a product and its potential impact on the market and come up with rather unique ideas as to how to promote and seize the opportunity.

Some other equipment companies had manufactured in-woods chipping machinery and various paper companies had experimented with debarking and chipping pulpwood on wood yards, but those efforts didn't stick so to speak.

"About 1967 I designed a portable debarker and chipper combination," Norval said. "The machine would debark treelength material and chip them. At that time, paper mills were looking for clean chips. Rather than cutting just roundwood and hauling it to the paper mill, they wanted the logs debarked and then chipped and they would rather accept a truckload of chips. That machine worked out fairly well. We probably sold 25 or 30 of them. They were quite a large machine and they were quite expensive."

Morbark called it the Chiparvestor, apparently named by marketing manager Bill Nelson. It was actually two pieces of equipment that were connected end to end, reaching about 100 feet in length. Morbark offered three models, with the largest going for about $120,000. Requiring only one operator, it included a hydraulic device called an F Stop, which was located ahead of the chipper infeed, and which automatically halted the infeed of logs whenever the chipper disc speed dropped below a certain level, helping to ensure consistent chip quality. The log loading mechanism consisted of hydraulic "ground line" arms located on each side of the debarker infeed conveyor. Log skidders dropped logs across the lowered arms, which would then elevate and roll the logs one at a time into the infeed conveyor to the debarker. The debarker itself was consistent with Morbark's debarking principle, operating with carbide tipped cutter teeth and giving the operator control of the infeed rate and cutting depth. The chipper was called Morbark's Golden Harvest, up to 75 inch. The design included an overhead discharge system with a swivel-type spout for blowing chips directly into chip vans. Bark was dispersed out the backside of the unit, where skidders could push it out of the way or use it to stabilize ground conditions. The debarker and chipper ran on separate diesel engines.

One paper company to try the largest Chiparvestor was Georgia Kraft Company, which bought and financed a Chiparvestor 2250 machine for a logger named Sam Fordham. (The 2250 meant the machine was designed to handle logs up to 22 inches in diameter and up to 50 feet in length.) The sale went through Morbark of Georgia and one of its representatives Jack Haygood. As Haygood recalled, near the end of 1967 an anxious Norval Morey was expecting a check from Georgia Kraft for the Chiparvestor, but Norval learned that the company had made it out to Morbark and Fordham, and placed it in the mail to Fordham. Norval contacted Haygood, said he needed the money, that development of the Chiparvestor was taking a financial toll, and told Haygood to retrieve the check. Haygood met with Fordham who endorsed the check after receiving it in the mail. Haygood flew to Michigan on December 23 and handed off the check (more than $100,000) to Norval.

The Chiparvestor wasn't overly successful, but it certainly wasn't a failure either, and it was a predecessor of much better things to come for Norval and Morbark with in-woods chipping equipment. What was immediately successful was Morbark's next product launch, a sawmill chipper called the Chip-Pac, which combined chipping, screening and a blower for loading chips into a trailer all on one common frame with the power unit. It initially sold for only $15,000, enabling owners of small sawmills to create value for slabs and edgings created during lumber manufacturing. The three-knife, 48 inch chipper was small enough to be tucked in a typical mill layout without costly building modification, could be set up in less than an hour, and required only a 40 HP motor. Morbark introduced it in August 1968 to 300 forest industry personnel at the plant in Winn. Dealers ordered it in bunches. The Chip-Pac was recognized as the Michigan Product of the Year for 1969 by the state's Department of Commerce.

Despite these rapid product developments and continuing expansion of the Morbark plant, it wasn't all work and no play. One of the more famous Norval Morey after-hour stories occurred at the Waldorf-Astoria Hotel in New York City during a meeting of the American Pulpwood Association. Morbark had a hospitality room together with equipment manufacturers Prentice and Timberjack, which allowed Norval to party with Leo Heikenen, the owner and developer of the Prentice loader, and Bill and Bob Bottoms, who helped to establish Timberjack. The partying had gone on long and room service was shut off. Norval and his buds sent out a few of the visitors to round up some food, and they returned with a crate of live chickens. They proceeded to butcher them in the room and attempted to roast them on a gas fired fireplace. One can only attempt to visualize the messy aftermath and Norval woke up the next morning fairly worried about having to pay a huge cleaning bill and possibly for other damages. When he went to the room he encountered the maid who had just finished cleaning it up. He apologized for the mess and asked what the manager of the hotel had said. But she told Norval she hadn't told any of the hotel staff. Norval gave her $100 and walked away relieved.

Norval's younger brother Harry, who was still managing the sawmill, liked to have a good time in his airplane. Once he took up his 14-year-old nephew Jerry Morey, going high over a heavily wooded area when suddenly the engine stopped. Harry started hollering for Jerry to locate a place to land the plane, then the plane started to nose dive before Harry started it back up.

In 1967, Morbark hosted a large gathering of its dealers when Harry and his plane appeared over the trees. The engine shut off and

Harry leaned out with a megaphone and shouted down to the crowd, "Cast your vote for George C. Wallace!" The plane then swooped underneath a power line, hit right in the middle of the road, bounded up and over a barbed wire fence and into a hayfield. When some of the crowd ran over there, many of them thinking Harry was a goner, they saw Harry and his plane mowing a path through the field and taking back off. Wallace, the former governor of Alabama, was running for president on the American Independent Party ticket. In 1972, when Wallace ran a second time, this time in the Democrat Party primaries, he carried the state of Michigan the day after he was shot and perma-

Hazel and Loyal came to know better times thanks to their son.

nently paralyzed while campaigning in Maryland.

The Morey family, and the community of Winn, suffered a heartfelt loss on May 8, 1967 with the death of Norval's mother, Hazel, at age 74. She had been living in a house across from the Morbark plant that Norval, Burnell and Harry had built for Harry, and where Harry lived until his family swapped residences with Hazel, who had been living in a country house built for her and Loyal a few miles away.

Her grandson Lon became close to her at about age 12 when he started helping her do chores around her house. "She became one of my best friends," Lon said. "She was a neat lady, a fat lady. She was a good cook, sewed a lot, would sit on her porch. She was always in her rocking chair. She was nosy. We had television but she would much rather listen to a neighbor's gossip."

Lon recalled the telephone party lines they had back then. "We were on there, Bardos was on there, Ralph was on there and a couple of others. Grandma always breathed real heavy. You knew she was on there because you could hear her breathing."

Her children, including Norval, jumped when she wanted something. More than once Norval would be in a meeting at Morbark when his secretary would enter and inform him that Hazel was on the phone. Norval's nephew Jerry recalled, "I'll never forget, we had a meeting going on, and the secretary comes into Norval's office and says, 'Hazel's on,' and he says, 'tell her I'm in a meeting,' and the secretary says, 'no, she said she's talking to you now.' Norval gets on the phone and you can hear her she talked so loud and she said, 'Norval, Tilly Williams and I and Gret want to go up to Burnell's cottage fishing cause we can get on his pontoon. Get somebody down here to take us.' Norval is embarrassed and I said 'I'll go find somebody to take them fishing.'"

Hazel experienced congestive heart ailments, at times worse than others, and she apparently expected to die sooner than she did. Left behind is a letter she wrote in cursive to her children dated December 30, 1963, more than three years before her death. Hazel could read, but her spelling was poor. The letter, as shown here, has been corrected for spelling.

December 30, 1963
Dear Children,
When you read this I will be gone. I don't want you to feel bad, for I have lived a full life and seen you all married with good homes, and I am proud of you and I know Dad would be too, and life hasn't meant so much to me since Dad has been gone.

You see I didn't make out a will for I thought you could settle it among you. Pay my bills and then settle it even among you children. Sell my home, and the note of Norval and Burnell can be cashed and I hope to have enough money in the bank to bury me. This is the way dad and I wanted it. Norval and I feel as if the price of the Family Monument should be taken out before you settle up.

All my love,
Ma

I would like Gret to have $100.00. She has earned it in being so kind to me and waiting on me.

I would like Burnell and Clara to have my bedroom suite.

All of Hazel's children had special memories of her, but certainly many of Norval's went back to his upbringing in the log cabin, helping his mom cook and do the laundry, the both of them realizing that Demlow School down the way wasn't for him beyond sixth grade. And for sure Norval gained some satisfaction in knowing that as a successful businessman he had been able to provide some comfort and leisure for Hazel in her elder years.

Hazel died on a Monday evening at Kelsey Memorial Hospital in Lakeview, leaving behind seven children, a sister, 24 grandchildren and 14 great grandchildren. She lay in state at her home, followed by funeral services at the Winn Methodist Church and burial at Union Cemetery, beside her husband and son.

The funeral not only attracted lots of Moreys, but more Moreys who were now working for Norval at Morbark. Leo's son, Larry, was following in his father's footsteps as plant manager, and now coming of age were Norval's son, Lon, Ralph's son, Mike, and Burnell's son, Jerry. But they were still young and learning the ropes, and weren't what Norval had in mind when he decided to go outside of the business to find a sales manager who could oversee and lead the company's booming growth (it now employed about 250) and continued expansion of its product offerings. After asking around, Norval came upon the name of Richard (Dick) Headlee. Headlee had been president of the U.S. Jaycees and more recently was an advisor to Michigan Governor George Romney and worked with the Romney for President Campaign. But when Romney bowed out of the race, Headlee needed a job. He had heard Morbark was looking for a sales manager and came to see Norval.

"He was really impressive," Norval said. "I could see right off the bat that he was really sharp and intelligent." Headlee wanted more than a sales manager title. He wanted to become the president of Morbark and help Norval run the company. Norval agreed, and Headlee came in and

hired several associates who came with him as part of his sales management team and as finance and credit managers. "Practically all of them
were real good people, except they didn't know much about our industry," Norval recalled. "But I gave Dick a lot of authority in the company
and right away he wanted to expand it; in my opinion too fast."

One of the moves Headlee made right away was to change Morbark's banking situation. Norval had dealt with the Old Kent Bank in
Grand Rapids for years, but Headlee moved the company's banking
interests to Manufacturers Bank in Detroit. And he borrowed a lot of
money, "three or four times as much money as we had ever borrowed
before," Norval recalled. Shortly after, Headlee led Morbark's purchase
of a struggling albeit long-time Oregon sawmill machinery manufacturer, Klamath-Ward. The purchase price was reportedly $400,000.
Headlee said in a statement, "Our addition of the Klamath-Ward line
now places Morbark Industries in the sawmill production line from the
log deck to the shipping dock. Klamath-Ward is just what we've been
looking for to ensure that Morbark will become one of the largest forest
industry machinery manufacturing complexes in the nation." While the
Oregon company's product line didn't really fit well with Morbark's,
Headlee's intent was to market and sell all of the Morbark products in
the Pacific Northwest and Western Canada through Klamath-Ward,
taking advantage of some tax writeoffs. But Headlee's new finance people hadn't done their due diligence on Klamath-Ward and liabilities
were greater than originally thought and the assets within the business
were greatly over-valued. The new acquisition quickly turned into a
money losing venture.

Another issue Norval said he had with Headlee was that Headlee
wanted to sell Morbark. "There was a company, Eaton, Yale and Towne,
that had bought Timberjack and paid a lot of money for it and they
were interested in buying Morbark," Norval said. Headlee thought it
was such a good deal that Norval should accept it. "It was several million dollars, but I wasn't interested in selling the company," Norval said.

Meanwhile Headlee was giving a lot of responsibilities at Morbark
to the new people he brought in, and this began to cause resentment.

Larry Burkholder, though promoted to vice president of sales and marketing by Headlee, and though he liked Headlee well enough, doubted that Headlee was doing the company any good. Burkholder and longtime salesman Jim Painter resigned in the fall of 1968 and moved to Tomahawk, Wis. to run a new Morbark dealership, Morbark of the Lake States. Their third partner was Norval.

Painter recalled when Norval said he would give Painter $10,000 if Painter could sell an original Chiparvestor that was sitting on the yard. Painter sold it and went into Headlee's office to collect. Headlee gave him a check for $5,000, but Painter countered that it should be $10,000. Headlee shook his head in disagreement. Painter motioned Headlee to follow him into Norval's office, where Painter asked Norval if he didn't promise $10,000 if Painter sold the machine. Norval confirmed it and Headlee wrote another check for $5,000. "Headlee never thought much of me after that," Painter said. "I never did think much of him."

The situation turned into a crisis when one of Norval's original right-hand men, Don Strong, came to Norval and said he wanted to quit. Strong was doing all the purchasing, running the stock room and lots of other jobs, and Norval never had to worry about him. Strong said he couldn't work for Headlee or one of Headlee's young new managers. Norval said he would see about removing the young manager and then Strong would only answer to Norval.

Norval recalled that he went to Headlee and told him they needed to get rid of the young manager, that he was causing too many problems and wasn't effective. But Headlee countered that Norval should look at the loan agreement Headlee had made with the bank in Detroit. It said that if Headlee or the young manager were discharged, this was grounds for the bank to pull the loan. Norval was flabbergasted, but didn't make a scene. "I just said, 'okay, if that's the way it is, I guess we'll keep him.'"

But, as Norval's nephew Jerry recalled, Norval faced quite a dilemma. Morbark was not in the greatest financial position at the time because of the costs that were incurred with the high priced management team that Headlee brought in, declining markets, and the financial strain that Klamath-Ward put on the business.

"That's when I went looking for another loan," Norval said. "But money was tight. It was very difficult to find a bank that would loan us a million and a half dollars, which at that time was an awful lot of money for the security that we had."

But Norval and his team, including Jerry, who worked for Morbark in accounting when he wasn't attending Central Michigan University, began talking with Prudential Insurance Company in Detroit. Norval recalled that when Headlee learned Norval was trying to secure a loan through Prudential, Headlee laughed about it because he didn't think there was any way Prudential would loan Norval the money to pay off the loan with the bank in Detroit.

When Prudential came up with a loan agreement, Norval gave it to Jerry to look over. Jerry was in his senior year in business/finance at the nearby university. When Jerry pointed out some things in the agreement such as warrants and stock options that he didn't think were appropriate, Norval told Jerry to meet with Prudential to see if he could get those items removed from the agreement.

"Keep in mind that I was a typical college student," Jerry recalled. "I went and bought a sports coat at Sears and a tie. At the time I had a Chevy that had slid into some mailboxes while I was delivering papers on my paper route. It wasn't pretty."

Norval gave Jerry a pep talk. "Go down there and be firm with those birds. Even though you are young, don't back down from them."

Jerry drove down to the Prudential office building where they had valet parking. "I didn't know there was such a thing as valet parking," he said. He walked into the lobby, asked for the loan manager and the receptionist made the call. About 15 minutes passed and Jerry went back up to the reception desk. Another call was made. After a few more minutes, a gentleman approached Jerry in the lobby. "Are you Norval Morey's financial advisor?" "I guess so," Jerry replied. The gentleman had come out to the lobby the first time but after looking around and seeing only this college student had departed. The loan officer led Jerry into the board room where five or six other other older gentlemen awaited. Jerry proceeded to go over the loan agreement and point out what he thought should be taken out and changed. "I was very forceful as Norval instructed me to be," Jerry said. "They sat there with their eyes wide open and didn't say a whole lot. They asked me financial questions and I responded to them."

The meeting lasted less than a half hour and they asked Jerry to return to the lobby and wait. After an hour, the loan officer came back and took Jerry to lunch. He told Jerry that he had never seen anybody pull anything like that. "I asked him what he meant," Jerry said. "He said that the Board was going to give Norval the loan, but they weren't going to take out any of the provisions that we asked to be removed. I told him that was all Norval wanted in the first place. He asked me to tell Norval one thing on behalf of the board. I asked what. He said, 'He has a lot of balls.'"

As soon as Norval received a telegram from Prudential congratulating him and Morbark on the loan, he set about dismissing Headlee and his team. Two stories persist as to how Headlee received the news. Years later Norval said he told Headlee himself, walking into Headlee's office and laying the telegram on Headlee's desk. Norval recalled, "He looked at it and almost turned white. He said, 'I'm very surprised. I didn't think they would ever loan the money.' I said, 'well, Dick, it's about 3 o'clock, do you suppose you and your other people can have everything gathered up around here that's your personal belongings by 5?' He jumped up and went to the three or four other people that he had hired and that's the way we ended doing business with him."

Jerry Morey recalled it differently. He said Norval didn't want to be around and asked Jerry to deliver the message to Headlee. Norval planned to be en route to a deer hunting outing in the Upper Peninsula. Norval had his attorney draft the letters of dismissal, and Jerry said Norval gave him instructions including the exact time Jerry was to approach Headlee. Norval was supposed to leave around 8:30 in the morning and Jerry was to dismiss Headley an hour later. Jerry said he informed Headlee at the designated hour, but actually Norval was still at the plant when it happened because one of the guys from the plant who was going to hunt with Norval couldn't get away as early as Norval wanted because of some work he still had to do at the plant.

No matter how it went down, Headlee departed the scene. He wasn't without work long, joining Alexander Hamilton Life Insurance Company and eventually becoming president and CEO in 1972. "He was a very intelligent man and a good talker," Norval said. Indeed Norval would cross paths with Headlee again in the not-too-distant future, and become a Headlee supporter.

Norval turned to members of the Morey family to fill some of the void left by Headlee and his cohorts. Norval gave his nephew Jerry a prominent role in sales and marketing and did likewise for his nephew Mike in the service department. He also put his son Lon over the parts department.

In fact Norval seemed to like it best when things were tough. He loved to bear down. Headlee's ouster presented Norval with the challenge of regrouping the company and Norval enjoyed the exercise immensely. Morbark was a dozen years old now and Norval had grown with it, developing his own leadership characteristics along the way. He was extremely passionate about his business and he had the knack for getting his employees fired up as well and believing in him. If one of his managers brought a new idea to him, he would challenge the manager and his idea to see how hard the manager would fight for the idea, and if the manager proved to be unbending and wholeheartedly committed, that would prove to Norval it was something that should be pursued. He wasn't beyond buying a manager an extra drink or two because he believed people talked a little bit more about what was really going on if they were loosened up. Sometimes these truth serum sessions might end up in an argument, and with Norval firing the worker, only to re-hire him.

Norval brought new ideas to the table as well, many of them following long weekends of giving it a lot of thought. Sometimes he would walk in Monday morning with sketches. His managers came to expect it and in one sense dread it, wondering if they would be altering something on the production line or in the marketing plan. He viewed himself as a vital part of research and development, and was capable in terms of designing equipment, and if he didn't design it, to come up with an idea as to the type or piece of equipment he wanted and how it would function and work with people in the shop in putting it together. He was the key person in product development. Many of Norval's ideas stuck, some of them didn't. Sometimes he would agree to a plan of action, but decide to change it without telling some of the managers who probably needed to know. He could be very impulsive, and sometimes he hadn't thought something through as much as he should have, and other times he was spot on. Some of his ideas left his managers shaking their heads, then down the road it would work out amazingly well.

He would let an employee come to his office at almost any time to discuss ideas or problems. If you went to him and he gave you his opinion, and if you didn't follow it, you wanted to be sure you made the right decision. And if you didn't take his advice and your action turned out wrong, you had better tell him the truth as soon as possible. He wasn't shy about reminding managers that he called the shots and it was his money on the line. He liked people who worked hard and sometimes rewarded them too much, putting them in a position beyond their capabilities, but usually his promotions proved to be the right move for the benefit of the employee and the betterment of the company.

Norval prided himself on being self-taught, but he saw the value in education. For a man who couldn't read very well, he was always trying to read something and comprehend it. He didn't like anybody wearing their higher education or their areas of specialization on their sleeves. Once when Morbark was hiring an engineer, the man went on about his degree and education. Norval leaned back in his chair and said, "I'll try not to hold that against you. I don't want to know about all your degrees. I just want to hear what you can do for us."

During a meeting you knew Norval was upset if he started rolling his tongue inside his cheek, and you knew he was really starting to burn up when he took off his glasses and started chewing on the stems. Generally he was slow to anger but if you kept harping on a subject he would get riled. When somebody mentioned that everybody was under a lot of stress, Norval would rear up, "What do you mean, stress? When you're sitting in a foxhole and you've been in there for two days and you can hear Germans talking within 200 feet and you know if you stick your head up…that's stress!"

His managers feared the beep on their phone systems when they saw it was coming from Norval. "Got a minute?" Norval would ask. They never were sure how to answer.

"Nub was very astute," recalled Larry Burkholder. "He usually had something in reserve. He was always thinking, working hard, playing hard, too. I think Norval would have been successful in any business. He was an entrepreneur."

Burkholder viewed himself as one of Norval's closest friends. "He and I fought. We worked together and played together. He told me a few times when he had been drinking, 'you're like a son to me, but you're not my son.'

"He wasn't one to put on airs. He knew who he was and didn't try to be anybody else. Most people liked the hell out of him because of the way that he would treat people and what he expected. He had that magnetism

Larry Burkholder knew Norval as well as anyone.

about him. I had a lot of admiration for him."

Their relationship was almost short-lived several years after Larry came to Morbark. They were flying in Norval's single engine plane down to Louisville, Mississippi to sign up Taylor Machine as a dealer and encountered thick fog in the area. The pilot started down to find the airport but it wasn't there and he brought the plane back up. He tried it again with the same result and told Norval in the co-pilot's seat and Larry in the back that they were about to run out of gas. Norval grabbed the map from the pilot as if to assume the navigation duties, upon which Larry smacked Norval in the shoulder and told him to give the map back to the pilot. The pilot said there it is and dipped down again, only with the same result. "I had seen the same cow three times," Larry recalled. The pilot came around again ready to land on what he thought was a road only to discover it was the ever missing runway. They happily walked three miles into town because the airport was closed.

Dealing with dealers was another characteristic of Norval's that sometimes left his employees scratching their heads, and Norval scratching his own. "He grew his business on having direct contact with the end user and got a lot of advice from them, and he lost some of that relationship when you put a dealer in the middle," Burkholder recalled. "That kind of bothered his philosophy of things. Norval always kept a certain amount of direct sales. When it got tight, dealers didn't want the inventory. He got frustrated with that."

Norval always felt that Morbark's machines were the primary reasons customers bought equipment, not so much the service and support that a dealer provided. He also thought the twenty percent discount a dealer might make was disproportionate to what Morbark was making off the sale. Especially with a patented product, like the whole tree chipper soon to come, when he had nearly all of the market, Norval felt he could sell them whether Morbark had dealers or not.

But when the market softened, and more sales and support punch was required to move machinery, he realized he needed some dealers. Norval's hot and cold relationship with dealers caused the Morbark sales department a lot of puzzlement and could send it scrambling at a moment's notice.

When wrestling with dealers and his own sales force began to irritate him, Norval would escape to the friendly confines of the factory, taking long walks through it, and stopping at many points along the way. The line workers respected him because he was friendly to them, could converse with them about the intricacies of the fabrication they were doing, and he didn't show off while he did it. He was also honest with them. If Morbark's business was off and it didn't look like things would pick up for a while, he told them the truth. He didn't hesitate to lend workers money, and usually never worried about collecting it back. What irritated him a little in the factory was to see small meetings going on, especially if he was in the dark about the subject matter. Sometimes he would say, "You know when I was in the Army, we kept from bunching up together so we wouldn't all get killed at the same time by a bomb." Somebody participating in one of those meetings might be summoned to Norval's office later in the day to answer a few questions and bring Norval up to date.

Norval loved building buildings and working with his brother-in-law Thurman on these projects. Morbark expanded again in 1968. Others in the company might have questioned why he was adding on, especially during weak markets, but Norval wanted the building and the manufacturing and storage capacity there when he needed it. Norval didn't worry too much about zoning requirements and permits. He once built an addition to Morbark on a county road without telling the county. Eventually the county came to him and said he couldn't do that without going through the proper procedures and gaining permission to re-route the road. "I didn't need to move it," Norval said. "I closed it."

As the 1970s approached, Norval had just turned 50 and still had a lot of energy, not only at work, but during social hour so to speak. He had smoked Winston cigarettes for many years, then when he developed lip cancer he tried smoking a pipe, only to return to cigarettes. His drinking was as strong as ever, and his tendency to drive fast hadn't waned either. Switching from a big green Chrysler, Norval had been driving two door hardtop Cadillac Eldorados for several years when he sped off Cold Water road, went down into a six foot ravine, tore out numerous small trees and shrubs on some private property before gaining control and getting the vehicle back on the road. The diversion tore up the oil pan and disfigured much of the vehicle. Norval got the car home into his garage and promptly called the local Cadillac dealer to bring him another identical one, which the dealer did while removing the old one. Nobody knew the difference until the property owners showed up a couple of weeks later to collect for damages.

Around the same period, Norval left a gathering at a bar in Winn and drove toward his home on Lake Isabella. His son, Lon, who was also at the bar, waited 15 minutes and followed his dad, who was not in the best of shape. Never seeing his dad's car, Lon assumed Norval had made it okay and Lon stopped at a bar at Lake Isabella. After Lon left the bar and headed back home, he came upon the blinking lights of a wrecker. Lon did a double-take when he saw the car that had run off the road and smashed head-on into a tree. It was his dad's car. Lon jumped out and the wrecker driver informed him that Bruce Welch, who was a Morbark employee, had taken Norval to the hospital and that Norval was alive. When Lon arrived at the hospital, he encountered an orderly sewing up Norval's knee, while Norval, still in good spirits, proclaimed he had sewn up many a trooper when he was in the service.

Everyone suspected that Norval was so intoxicated and his body so limbered that the impact had merely tossed him around harmlessly inside the car like a bouncing ball. However, his knee was never quite right again.

Later on, Norval had another accident in an Eldorado on Highway 131 near his cottage on the Muskegon River. It wasn't his fault. The other driver had been drinking or fallen asleep and slammed Norval head-on. Air bags saved Norval in that one. The word going around the Morbark plant and the Winn community was that "Norval Morey was still living that charmed life."

Pretty soon the nation's forest products industry was saying the same thing, as Norval and Morbark embarked on a venture that forever changed the landscape and status quo of the wood fiber supply chain and vaulted Morbark Industries to a new level of annual revenue.

Several circumstances in the late 1960s led to the creation of what would become Morbark's signature product—the whole tree chipper (WTC). Dutch elm disease had spread rapidly in major cities in the upper Midwest and southern Ontario. North American elms were very susceptible to the disease, first encountered in the Netherlands in the early '20s and first detected in the U.S. around 1930 in Cleveland, Ohio, where it evidently arrived in a log shipment from Europe. The disease had killed millions of elm trees worldwide by 1970. Dozens of municipalities found themselves dealing with a challenging problem in the disposal of dead trees.

At the same time, a growing number of local and state governments, under pressure from environmental groups, were passing laws banning the open burning of debris generated in land clearing operations and construction projects. Also, the Environmental Protection Agency was nearing its beginning during the first Nixon Administration. Municipalities, tree care companies and land clearing contractors were being forced to turn to landfills for disposal of dead and downed tree trunks, branches and stumps. Landfills accepted this waste reluctantly because the bulky products took up lots of space, shortening their lifespan. Related transportation costs and tipping fees were costly. All parties involved were eager for a lower cost solution.

Meanwhile, during the Headlee period Norval had permanently shut down the Morey sawmill. Norval and brother Harry, the mill manager, subsequently formed a Winn-based dealership known as Morbark Logging Equipment, which sold and serviced Morbark machinery in Michigan, Ohio, Indiana and Illinois. It also carried Timberjack skidders, Bombardier logging and snow removal equipment, Taylor forklifts and Titan chain saws. The business had two outside salesmen, Ray Billsby, Harry's brother-in-law, and Pete Radcliff, who had called on the Moreys for years as a representative of both Bombardier and Titan. Radcliff, in his Morbark Logging Equipment role, routinely engaged park and recreation department heads as he promoted Bombardier and Titan products. Urban tree companies were routinely using brush chippers to get rid of small trees and branches, but some of them knew of the Morbark Chiparvestor system and its ability to chip large, long logs. They told Radcliff they needed a machine that could chip an entire tree to help them deal more effectively with dead elm trees. If nothing else, chips could be used as mulch, or, if dumped in a landfill, they would take up less space than logs and limbs.

Radcliff recalled, "It was Harry who convinced Norval that he should get an engineer involved in designing something to crush the limbs down on the tree so that it would pass through the chipper." The story goes that Norval at first resisted, perhaps because a previous big ticket item, the Chiparvestor system, had not been a major success, but more likely because he wasn't infatuated with marketing his products to large cities. "I don't think Nub had much love for cities and people who were not in the wood products industry," Radcliff said. "If his equipment was going to be used by a city, he was okay with it, but he wasn't crazy about selling it to them."

But as utility construction companies and urban maintenance departments continued to express their need for a machine, Norval and Harry began to think of the potential market for it—not only those requesting it now, but also for the production of in-woods chips that went to making building products such as particleboard and flakeboard, and perhaps even pulp and paper. Norval called in the company's best engineer, Lee Smith, whom Larry Burkholder was instrumental in hiring from a fabrication firm in Saginaw a few years earlier in order to design and manufacture some feeding and handling equipment to accompany the company's debarkers into sawmills. Smith didn't have a degree in engineering, but he was a heck of a draftsman who had engineering skills.

What they came up with was an apparatus that was well suited for handling bark laden trees with broken and bent branches, trees with crooked trunks and trees with leafy foliage, an apparatus that could crush and fold the branches to the trunk of the tree without the branches springing back as they entered the chipper. The feed assembly conveyed the tree butt end first and a power driven upper drum roll cooperated with a conveyor for conveying the tree toward the chipping unit while folding the branches vertically inward toward the tree trunk. A pair of upstanding side rolls were positioned to form a throat for also engaging the tree branches. For driving the drum, a sprocket wheel was fixed to a supporting shaft and a chain was trained around the sprocket wheel and another sprocket wheel was driven by the output shaft of a hydraulically operated rotary motor supported on the transverse beam. The drive roll, conveyor chain and upstanding rolls funneled the trees forward into the feed chute of the chipper, which was a rotatable chipping disc driven by a power source such as a diesel engine.

Smith is listed as the inventor of this machine, and Morbark Industries the assignee on the U.S. patent that was filed for in January 1971 and issued in May 1972. When Norval filed for the patent, the machine was actually called the Tree Destroyer.

But the prototype machine was dubbed the Metro Chiparvestor. It came together quickly and required very few modifications—quite amazing considering there were no prints to go by. "We had everything we needed but a hydraulic loader, so that helped move things along," recalled Radcliff, who emphasized that the development was a prime example of free enterprise com-

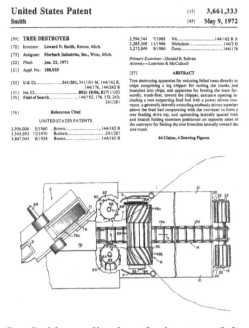

Lee Smith was listed as the inventor of the Tree Destroyer.

bined with entrepreneurial spirit. He remembered a salesman for Drott Manufacturing Company once telling him how he envied Morbark's fast, albeit loose way of getting things done. Radcliff asked the man to elaborate: "Hell, if Nub scratches out something on a napkin at lunch, they're building it that afternoon."

Soon municipal and tree care company representatives from Detroit, Chicago and Toledo and numerous land clearing contractors were coming to Winn to watch demonstrations. All were impressed. Chicago officials kept pushing Radcliff for the price of the machine and he kept pushing Norval. Radcliff recalled, "Finally, Norval said, 'Well, how many pounds do we have there?' and I told him I didn't know. He said, 'I'll figure it out.' When he got around to it he priced it at $89,500, which was about $2 a pound. The city of Chicago accepted the final price and went ahead and bought it." Chicago probably purchased the second machine. The first purchase apparently went to

PennLine, a utility construction company, in July 1970.

Weighing about 44,000 pounds, the four-wheeled, highway tow-able Metro featured a 75 inch, 3-knife, 6-inch thick disc chipper with 22-inch tree diameter capacity; a chip blower; a Prentice GOBC hydraulic loader and 310 horsepower Cummins engine. A lone operator, seated on the loader, fed trees to the machine.

Morbark formed a Metro Division not long after the product was introduced and Norval hired Jack Cavanaugh to manage it. He convinced Norval that the most effective way to sell the machines was to hire recently retired, well known sports celebrities and make them responsible for a specified region. Cavanaugh hired Milt Plum, former quarterback for the Detroit Lions; Gail Cogdill, All-Pro wide receiver for Detroit and later Baltimore; and Steve Barber, a 15-year pro baseball pitcher, primarily for the Orioles. Radcliff traveled with each and helped with their training. He recalled that Plum was the most industrious and successful of the three, but that overall the sports celebrity sales scheme fizzled out. Morbark and Plum went to court over compensation Plum thought he was due. Plum was living in North Carolina, and Burt Carlson, procurement manager with Champion International from North Carolina, said to Norval, "Let me tell you something. You're going to go into that North Carolina court looking for justice and come out begging for mercy." "And that's what happened," recalled Larry Burkholder, who wasn't allowed to take the stand during an abbreviated trial.

The Metro Chiparvestor was hot for a season but sales slowed once the limited municipal market was saturated. And, as it turned out, not that many tree service or land clearing companies were yet willing to part with $90,000 for a single purpose, newfangled machine. But Norval and Harry saw the larger potential for the machine, and that paper, paperboard and composite board manufacturers would be interested in the whole tree concept, particularly now as the demand for pulp and paper was strong but wood supplies were short, especially in the South which had experienced significant rainfalls. Norval saw all of this unfolding and was determined that a lot of low grade pulp mills could use undebarked chips.

A Michigan field trial in the spring of 1971 was among the first to attract scores of curious woodlands managers and wood fiber procurement officials for forest products and paper companies. The whole tree chipper was rolled out and included a screen that discarded oversized pieces and much of the undersized contaminant material before the chips were blown into a van. The harvesting component during the demonstration included a Drott feller-buncher and two Timberjack grapple skidders, which worked in unison with the chipper to produce tons of hardwood chips in minutes. This probably was the event that caught the attention of *Pulpwood Production* magazine, which in August 1971 devoted its cover and two inside pages to the revolutionary development that Morbark branded as "Total Chips." The article noted the trial's significant gain in wood fiber recovery per acre over conventional harvesting methods. It also noted that Norval believed the Total Chips scheme opened a way to a more complete utilization of the nation's timber resource. "We can no longer afford to waste one third to one half (of a stand's fiber) through littering and burning," he was quoted as saying. The article also included a telling statement from J. H. McCleod, wood-chip procurement manager for Masonite Corp., Laurel, Miss.: "Increased yield is only part of the benefit of the concept. Another is that it leaves the land clean and ready for replanting. It virtually eliminates site preparation and related costs." Further, the article noted that a paper sample Morbark claimed was made from Total Chips was "hardly distinguishable" from paper made from chips processed in the test mill's conventional wood room.

Morbark expanded these impressive demonstrations across several months and at various locations in the Lake States, South and Northeast, producing chips for testing at numerous plants that manufactured a variety of products. Wood procurement agents were intrigued by the productive capacity of the Total Chips system. Several mills conducted in-plant tests, blending whole tree chips with more sanitized chips developed conventionally at mill wood yards. For the most part, the results were generally favorable. Morbark's participation in a conference of the Technical Association of the Pulp and Paper Industry in 1972, where Westvaco

Corporation personnel told of successful experiments with whole tree chips, helped enliven the phenomenon. Even so, some mill engineers were wary of contamination from inherent grit, dirt and bark and the damage they could inflict on sensitive machine systems; marketing people were likewise concerned with how the comparatively unrefined whole tree chips might impact, or appear to impact, product quality.

Harry Morey started his own logging company, Total Chips, Inc., in 1971. Harry said, "I wanted to go into business for myself to prove what the machine would do; that it would increase utilization of raw material from a given tract and make a true selective thinning of hardwoods and other species economically feasible for the first time." Harry was speaking the same language as Norval on this one, but they were speaking less and less to each other. Harry probably felt he deserved more recognition for his contributions to the company through the years, but Norval was slow on such recognition and the older brother was increasingly irritated by the younger brother. But Harry's role in the marketing of the whole tree chipper was crucial to its early success. In May 1971 Harry delivered 2,500 tons of hardwoods, mostly oak, to S. D. Warren Paper in Muskegon, which wanted to test run the chips for paper making. "They were the first company to use total tree chips in paper making," Harry said. Paper company after paper company visited Harry's logging operation and came away sold on the machine.

For a couple of years after he left Morbark, Harry exploited his ties with the company and his brother, occasionally bounding in and helping himself to parts, steel and other items without paying for them. If someone questioned him Harry would simply refer the frustrated questioner to Norval. Larry Burkholder recalled, "One time Harry drove up out back after hours and started loading some steel. A night watchman rushed up to Harry and asked him what he was doing. 'I'm stealing steel,' Harry said indifferently, and continued building the load. When told about the incident, Norval just laughed." Harry set up his logging shop behind his home in nearby Shepherd—the same home where Hazel and Loyal had lived.

Morbark went from selling one or two whole tree chippers a month in 1971 to one per week in early 1973. Norval decreed that the Total Chiparvestor—its rebranded name—would take priority at the factory.

Whole tree chipper demand soared in 1973 and continued well into 1974, not only driven by markets for making paper, but also by the Arab Oil Embargo, which shocked U.S. energy markets and led numerous paper and paperboard mills to begin burning more wood, including whole tree chips, and less fossil fuels in their in-plant heat energy systems. The success of the machine prompted Morbark to start up a new publication, *What's new in Total Chip Harvesting*. The publication featured a page that listed mill customers and the number of Total Chiparvestors they owned and operated or that were operated by loggers for supplying their mills. In mid 1974 the publication reported 185 machines in operation and less than a year later showed 250. The biggest mill customers were Westvaco, Weyerhaeuser, Georgia-Pacific and Masonite. Private landowners welcomed whole tree chipping as well, as the value of their timber resource was increased, and the leftover condition of the land made it easier and more economical for landowners to reforest or convert the land to another use.

After sagging in 1970-71, Morbark sales had recovered to around $7 million mark in 1972 and reached nearly $15 million the next year. Revenues were projected to hit a whopping $40 million in 1974. By this time Morbark had expanded its plant to 538,000 square feet—more than 12 acres under one roof—and was once more expanding with a 228,000 square foot project under way. To keep up with Total Chiparvestor demand, Norval suspended the production of all sawmill equipment in favor of whole tree chippers, and set up a 422-foot assembly line. Beside this line was the chipper assembly line, its output coordinated to hand off completed chippers to the appropriate station on the Total Chiparvestor line. The company in mid-1974 was turning out one Total Chiparvestor per day—the most popular of now several models being the Model 22. Its price had increased to about $95,000. A fleet of trucks owned and maintained by the company delivered the machines to customers. The company also completed construction of new office facilities of nearly 14,000 square feet.

Thurman Barrett and Norval always seemed to have an expansion project in the works.

Morbark concurrently launched a series of three-day seminars on whole tree harvesting for small groups at its headquarters in early 1974. It gradually began incorporating owners of Total Chiparvestors into the program to talk about their specific operations and conditions and subsequently began holding the seminars at various locations in the U.S. and Canada. Morbark gradually worked in discussions on economics, conservation, the environment and new developments from other noncompetitive equipment manufacturers.

Norval took a big picture approach and became very aggressive in promoting the improvement of the country's forest resources for future generations, emphasizing that the best way to go about it was to utilize the forests through proper management and harvesting techniques and methods, whether the prescription called for clear-cutting, select-cutting or thinning, especially on privately owned timberlands that lacked intensive forest management. Morbark pushed what it now called The Total Chiparvestor System, which of course called for the use of the company's whole tree chipper.

A roaring economy in 1973 worked for and against Morbark and other makers of heavy machines in that it created tight supplies of steel. Morbark's heavy chipper discs were built with six inch plates. Jerry Morey recalled, "We couldn't get enough of it to meet demand. We probably bought some black market stuff. Some of it was no good and we had to throw it out." The federal government was trying to get a handle on what kind of import and export policies and restrictions it should implement for steel, but this only tended to make the chain of supply more erratic. This circumstance, combined with Norval's tendency to save manufacturing costs by not overbuilding, prompted him to tinker with a redesign of the chipper disc, working with Lee Smith to eventually come up with what was called the Trigon Disc. It wasn't as thick or as heavy-duty as the original circular chipper disc that was in the Total Chiparvestor, and the result was less efficient production. After about a year, Morbark returned to original chipper disc. About the only other issue in the Total Chiparvestor setup was the knuckleboom loader, which Morbark was purchasing and setting up to the chipper. In addition to maintenance issues, it gave the loader operators too much leeway in handling the trees, resulting in some weight balance problems.

Morbark's whole tree chipper revolutionized the forest industry.

Norval then conceived the slide-boom loader as a cure, which basically dummied down the loading and feeding of the trees, making it very straightforward with little margin for error.

In May 1974 Ron Poparello left Newark, NJ and came aboard as vice president of finance, leaving the national accounting firm of Arthur Anderson. He encountered boom times at Morbark Industries along with lofty machine sale and revenue projections. "Norval had put together this very attractive bonus program that included all the employees in the company." Poparello said. "Everybody was receiving big monthly bonuses. I went there on May 1 and I got a nice bonus for the month of May."

Poparello said while Norval could certainly have a dominating personality, he could be extremely kind to people. "He wasn't the kind of guy you could demand something of because you felt you were entitled to it; it was more that he would give it to you because he wanted you to have it."

But Poparello recalled that suddenly the good times ended, especially when a major paper company came out with a report that the whole tree chips which Morbark was promoting were dirty and contaminating their paper making equipment. The company killed its order of a half dozen whole tree chippers. "From that moment on we probably got as many cancellations as we got orders," Poparello said. "It turned out to be a real dismal period." After annual revenue reached $25 million in 1974, it declined to seven million dollars in 1975, and layoffs ensued.

"I think Norval's attitude was things will turn out," Poparello recalled. "He was optimistic but at the same token he was certainly uninhibited in terms of making changes in personnel and putting in paycuts."

That summer when Poparello planned to go on vacation, he received word from Mike Morey, whom Norval had put in charge of whole tree chipping manufacturing, that the company couldn't afford to pay Poparello while he was on vacation. Poparello canceled his trip.

Norval pushed forward. Poparello recalled they met with the bank in Detroit because they wanted some additional credit and more flexibility in their lending terms. At first the bank refused, but Norval was adamant. "I didn't think we were negotiating from a position of strength, but I learned otherwise. Norval told them we would take our business elsewhere and look for a new banking relationship, and by the time we reached the elevator they had changed their mind and decided they could do some of the things that Norval wanted to do."

Paper companies approached the issue of whole tree chips in different ways, though most recognized that in-woods chips was becoming a fixture in the wood fiber supply chain. Some pulp operations were more aggressive than others in trying to adapt their mill machinery to in-woods chips for producing Kraft linerboard for cardboard packaging. Norval also recognized that in-woods chips produced by his Total Chiparvestor required additional screening and separation to remove bark percentage and other contaminants to make truly grade pulp chips. He came up with the Class-A-Fiber System, basically a secondary chip processing satellite mill. Vans filled with chips would be brought in, stationed in a semi-circle and unloaded with a traveling scooper, which deposited the chips to a screening system and separated out oversize material to a rechipper before being fed back to the screen. These chips then moved to a second screen where fines were screened out and from which "Class A" chips for high grade paper were transferred into outgoing vans or rail cars. The system offered subsequent screening stations for the separation of descending grades of chips.

Norval said, "I am satisfied that the final chapter has been written on experimentation, with the results being a sophisticated system which combines air separation with a series of hexagon drums screens. We are very enthusiastic about the results this system produces, as we find that total chips can be processed through the Class-A-Fiber System and produce the highest quality chips yet to be found from any previous system."

The Class-A-Fiber System didn't catch on as totally designed, though the concept of additional screening and materials separation did. However, the matter of sufficient bark removal still reared its head, and Norval and Morbark continued to wrestle with it. They soon made a simple and successful addition to their whole tree chipper, called the Dirt Separator, which was a partition device that separated out bark, sand and grit from the tree as it was being chipped.

The uncertainty of some paper mills concerning the quality and manufacturing ramifications of in-wood chips may have contributed to a momentary setback for Morbark's Total Chiparvestor. But perhaps equally as hindering was the energy crisis in America, brought on by the OPEC oil embargo during 1973-1974. Initially, as oil and gas prices escalated as a result of the embargo, paper mills started burning more wood to create power for their plants, contributing to sales of the Total Chiparvestor for producing low grade fuel chips with little worry over matters such as bark content. But as the crisis persisted and grew worse, with long lines at gas stations becoming routine, the economy's purchasing power and manufacturing momentum dwindled across the board to a very slow drip. America went into a recession. Manufacturing shut down. In his office at Morbark, Norval began to think long and hard about how to turn the energy crisis into an opportunity not only for Morbark but for the entire forest industry.

In addition to his whole tree chipper, Norval figured part of some kind of energy harvesting formula would include the tree shear Morbark had introduced a couple of years earlier. Drott Manufacturing, owned by Norval's friend, Erv Drott, had operated a scissor-type felling device attachment on Drott's track type excavator during those Morbark whole tree chipping demonstrations for pulp and paper mills. But the machine was relatively slow. Norval wanted something lighter, quicker and more affordable, and turned to Morbark's Lee Smith. Soon a 15 inch capacity shear evolved and proved effective in tests as an attachment on the Melroe Bobcat skid steer carrier. Morbark subsequently introduced its feller-buncher attachment in 1973 and soon added several models of varying capacities that could be fitted on many types of carriers, including skid steer tractors, front-end loaders and excavators. Morbark was among the first to offer a felling head that could continue to cut, accumulate and hold several trees before dumping them in a neat pile, where a tractor or skidder could easily grab them and drag them to the landing for chipping or loading onto trucks.

Norval was constantly thinking about other opportunities as well. He set out to find a partner who could build and market a chipper knife line. Morbark had tested several brands of chipper knives but with little satisfaction, except for the knives produced by United Shoe Machinery in Medway, Massachusetts. Norval met Jay Halloran, who was the division manager, and some months later, with Norval's resources and Halloran's knowhow, they started Michigan Knife Company and began building a plant in a vacated 70,000 square foot building in Big Rapids, Michigan. During 1974 and 1975 Michigan Knife primarily produced knives for Morbark Industries and Canadian Morbark of North Bay, Ontario, Canada. As the market condition softened in the wood industry, it became apparent that Morbark's business alone couldn't keep Michigan Knife operating at its capacity. Several employees from Halloran's former company joined Morbark and helped to establish a West Coast sales and distribution branch, and it proved to be highly successful. Emphasis then turned to the East Coast market, including the introduction of a knife grinder, which was shown at a wood products industry expo in New Orleans. By 1980 the company was poised for additional growth and the expansion of its manufacturing plant and its product line.

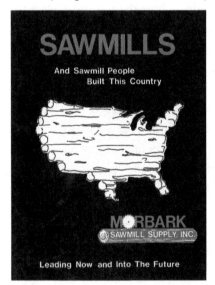

When people thought of Morbark, they thought of debarkers and chippers, but the company continued to promote, and with success, its other sawmill equipment and accessories.

As hectic and thrilling as the first half of the 1970s was for Norval with regard to his business, his personal life was as equally traumatic and some of it tragic. On June 5, 1971 Norval lost his older brother Burnell to lung cancer at age 55. Burnell died at the Butterworth Hospital in Grand Rapids. The funeral service and burial were held at St. Leo's Catholic Church and Cemetery in Winn. Burnell left behind his wife, Clara, four sons and two daughters. Another daughter, Linda Ann, had died of a rare strain of hepatitis in 1968 at age 19. Burnell's four brothers and two sisters still survived him. It was of course Burnell who had formed the early working partnerships with Norval, first as fallers through several logging seasons in the Northwest and then after the war in the formation of Morey Brothers Sawmill. During the war Burnell, as did Norval, saw more than his share of combat, plowing through France and Germany as part of a tank regiment and as the leader of a tank squadron.

Later in 1971, on October 14, Norval's brother-in-law, Andy Bardos (Lucille's husband), died at age 47 from complications stemming from Huntington's Chorea, a prolonged neurodegenerative, genetic disorder. Andy had worked with the Morey brothers at the beginning, and two of his sons, Jim and Gary, played important roles in parts and fabrication at Morbark throughout the years.

Norval's son, Lon, and Lon's wife at the time, Linda, lost boy and girl twins at birth in 1973. And an extremely tragic accident took the life of Norval's grandson, Jeffrey Tice, Betty's son, at age six in the summer of 1975. Betty recalled the relationship between her son and her dad. "Jeff was close to my dad; he looked so much like him. I remember when dad had bought a brand new pontoon and Jeff was down there fishing and he got his fish pole caught on the fringe of the boat. And my dad took a knife and cut it out and he dropped the knife. Jeff took the knife and was poking holes in the seat and dad went down and spanked him. My little boy didn't shed a tear and he said, 'that didn't hurt.' Dad had to get off the boat he was laughing so hard. He just loved little Jeff and all the little kids." Betty's brother Lon recalled that their father was active in raising Jeff and was very attached to him and Jeff's older sister, Tracy.

Betty was out of town when a friend, Judy, drove Jeff, Tracy, a woman minister and another young lady from the church to go roller skating in St. Louis. Afterward, on their way back home, four miles outside of Winn, a drunk driver missed a curve and crashed head-on into their car. Jeff and Judy, the driver, were killed. Tracy suffered serious head injuries, from which she recovered. The other driver was also killed.

Later at the funeral when Norval saw the boy lying in-casket, neatly groomed, Norval ran his hand through the boy's hair and messed it up a little. "Jeff's hair was never combed," Norval said as he welled up.

Norval's reputation was one of taking care of his family members. When his sister Lucille went out West with a second husband and experienced some domestic difficulties, Norval brought her and her children back to the more relaxing environment of Winn. Certainly through the years Norval saw to it that various family members had a house to live in.

In 1969, Norval and Phyllis moved into a big house of their own on Lake Isabella. Norval and Thurman Barrett designed the sprawling three-story home. In order to have a tennis court and have ample space for his flowers and vegetable garden, Norval purchased the lots on either side of the house, along with the one across the street. People for miles around came to view the long rows of bright impatiens Norval planted each year. So massive was the annual planting, the flowers could be seen by passing aircraft. The Lake Isabella Golf Course was within walking distance and Norval played some rounds there. (About this time Norval also took to snow skiing as he expanded his recreational endeavors beyond hunting, which he continued to excel in as well.) The house also featured an indoor pool made to look like an icy cavern and a party room with a full bar and stereo system. But while Norval and Phyllis continued to make a great team in entertaining and feeding their guests, in private their relationship had greatly deteriorated.

Some years later when Norval was considering publishing a book on his experiences—an exercise that barely got out of the planning stages—he spoke on tape about his declining relationship with Phyllis, and that it had been in demise for some years before they moved into the new house. Norval was quick to praise Phyllis as an excellent mother of their children and as a host to their friends and Norval's business guests. But Norval referred to Phyllis as a negative person. "On almost anything you could suggest, at first she would be against it," he said. "She would criticize other people for no reason that I could see. And I never liked that attitude. As she got older it seemed to me that problem kept getting worse. I just didn't want to put up with that the rest of my life."

Norval said he told her some years earlier that once the kids were grown he would separate from her, though continue to support her financially. He doubted whether Phyllis believed he would go through with it. He told his son Lon of his intentions about the time Lon was graduating from high school.

Norval and Phyllis were still together when Norval decided to build the new house. At first he was looking at a site near the plant, but then he liked what he saw at Lake Isabella and bought four lots. "I built a very expensive house for those days, probably as good a house or maybe the best house in the county," he recalled. He asked Phyllis to shop around and pick out the furniture but in the end they looked around together and picked it out. It included a cherry dining room suite, walnut bedroom suite and other high end items, but Norval said Phyllis was never happy with the furniture or the new house. Finally he told her he was ready to move out and she could stay in the new house, or he could stay in it and buy her a house to live in. Phyllis preferred to move out, first living in a condo in Mount Pleasant and then moving into a house. "I think she was quite bitter," Norval said. "Not so much that she loved me, but because of maybe a failure (in not being able to make the marriage work)."

Norval and Phyllis divorced in March 1977 after 31 years of marriage. They would continue to visit with each other now and then and sometimes have dinner. But by then another woman, and her two children, had entered Norval's life.

Michelle White was 10 years old in 1973 when, following her parents' bitter divorce, she and little sister Julie came from Southern California to the Isabella County community of Riverdale with their mother, Jeri McCall, who had relatives in the area. Jeri wanted the girls to grow up in a more wholesome environment than could be found in Los Angeles. When they arrived in Isabella County, Jeri had a decade of secretarial experience under her belt, the most recent being with a large company in Beverly Hills. She eventually landed a position at Morbark, which was about 12 miles from their new home in Gratiot County.

Within a year, Jeri and Norval began seeing each other, though Norval and Phyllis were still married. When the relationship became serious, Norval moved the two girls and their mother to Traverse City for the sake of their privacy. "There was a lot of gossip when they started dating," Michelle said. "It was big news all over the Winn area. We were in a very small, tight-knit community and I think all the talk made Nub and my mom uncomfortable. Nub decided we could have more anonymity in Traverse City than in Riverdale."

Norval soon found out that Jeri had a mental illness known as bipolar disorder. The illness caused extreme mood swings, from mania to depression. A person experiencing an euphoric mania episode seldom sleeps, behaves with great peculiarity to the point of losing touch with reality, and can even endanger his or herself or others because of this extreme behavior. Jeri, like many sufferers, could grow abusive, and as a result Norval and others close to her suffered extreme emotional stress as they tried to rein her in. Her mood swings could send the otherwise happy lakeside home into pandemonium and send everyone running for cover. She would blast Neil Diamond songs from the stereo in the middle of the night and lash out at people for no reason. Once, while on a cruise with Norval's eldest daughter Connie, Jeri became so unruly, the two of them were put off of the ship in Tahiti. Norval had to send an employee to go and retrieve them.

"Dad didn't know what to do with her illness," Michelle said. "But he made some good decisions on her behalf." Norval had Jeri examined at Mayo Clinic in Rochester, Minnesota, where a new medicine was prescribed. It worked well, as long as she continued to take it. The lithium medication leveled off her emotions, but when she quit taking it, the episodes started again.

Norval's daughter Betty recalled, "I have to give credit to my dad. Many people would have said 'I can't deal with it' and be done with it. But my dad dealt with it."

Norval's daughter Connie seemed to get along okay with Jeri, but Betty's relationship with Jeri was more strained and Betty felt threatened when Jeri was in the middle of an episode. Bipolar disorder is believed to be genetic to some degree and an episode tends to kick in due to a major emotional situation in one's life.

Norval and Phyllis divorced in March of 1977. He and Jeri were married in Las Vegas one month later and along with Jeri's daughters lived at the new Lake Isabella home. "I am so glad he was part of my life," Michelle said. "He was very good to us. We always felt protected with dad, felt taken care of and we miss him terribly."

White described her home life as lively. Norval and Jeri hosted family, friends and customers. He and Jeri enjoyed dancing with each other and liked the same kinds of music. The B.J. Thomas mega hit, "Raindrops Keep Falling On My Head," was one of their favorites. Norval liked to cut flowers from his garden, arrange them and bring them in to present to Jeri. "They really adored each other," Michelle said of the pair. "He loved to have mom read aloud to him."

Norval enjoyed discussing the political events of the day with his girls. He even came to show a rare silly side with his new daughters. He would bring home frog legs to cook for dinner and put on this puppet show with them. "It broke us up. I don't think he showed that side to many people," Michelle said.

"As successful as he was, he was never high and mighty," Norval's step-daughter said. "He was a very humble man. He would come home from the office with a big smile on his face and take that hoe out to his flowers or his vegetable garden. That hoe represented my dad more than anything else he owned."

"She was a beautiful woman," Larry Burkholder recalled of Jeri Morey. "She was the love of Nub's life but he had a hard time dealing with her during the bad times."

At home and at work, Norval Morey had a lot on his plate during the latter half of the 1970s, and the more that was piled on, the better he seemed to perform.

FOUR

O'Connor Creative Services
North Hollywood, California
November, 1978

Ronald Reagan arrived at the O'Connor Creative Services studio, entered the recording room, tossed his jacket on an adjacent chair and sat down in front the microphone. He waved through the large glass at the pretty young lady on the other side of it. She stood next to a young man sitting at the control panel. The man waved at Reagan without looking up as he continued to toy with the knobs and levers. The young lady, holding a clipboard, smiled at Reagan—a smile Reagan had seen thousands of times; well, not really a smile, more of a blush and a blink of the eyes followed by the hand brushing a few strands of hair off the forehead. This was how girls had reacted to him for years, and frankly he was glad to see they still did. "I suppose once a movie star, always a movie star," he said to himself with a grin as he picked up the papers next to the microphone.

"Did you say something Governor Reagan?" the man asked, now smiling at Reagan. The young lady behind him was smiling as well.

"Just talking to myself, Harry." Reagan said, knowing full well they had heard him. "Old habit I picked up when I was in the movies. It keeps getting me in trouble." Harry was Harry O'Connor, the owner of the studio who was gaining somewhat of a reputation for syndicated radio shows of a *politically conservative nature. In addition to Reagan, Efrem Zimbalist, Jr. was doing a series with O'Connor, as was Art Linkletter.*

"Okay governor, give me a few lines to check our levels," the young man said.

"Reagan sat up and leaned toward the microphone. "My fellow Americans, I'm pleased to announce that I've signed legislation outlawing the Soviet Union. We begin bombing in five minutes."

O'Connor smiled as he adjusted the controls. The young lady giggled. Both O'Connor and Reagan looked at her with surprise, then looked at each other and nodded at the young lady's sense of humor, which heretofore hadn't surfaced. "Dear, I may have a place for you in my administration," Reagan said. The young lady blushed again.

He was in his fourth year of recording these radio broadcasts, having started them even before he ran for the Republican Party nomination for president in 1976. He expected them to continue for another year until he kicked his presidential campaign into full gear for the 1980 election. And, God willing, when he resumed them again he would be sitting in the White House recording room as president of the United States.

He glanced through his pile of broadcast scripts. He would be reading 10 of them today and they would air during the next several weeks over more than 300 stations to thirty million listeners. As usual, he would need only one take for each of them. Talking into a microphone was as natural to Reagan as, well, kissing a leading lady. He had written his scripts in long hand, read through them as he timed himself with a stopwatch, made some changes and read through them again until he had whittled them down to the three minutes given him. He dropped them off at the studio for Harry to edit and type up. He separated two of the scripts from the others and glanced through them. "Let's start with Wood and Norval Morey," he said.

He pictured the man in his mind. Bushy eyebrows, a thick mustache with a lot of black and gray in it, hair messed up a little and combed over, a rounded face. Reminded Reagan a little of Yogi Berra, except for the mustache. Norval Morey had worn a nice suit when he came to Reagan's office in Chicago about two weeks earlier. They had met a couple of times before, once even before Reagan's unsuccessful run in 1976. Norval Morey wasn't shy about writing a check, Reagan thought. He had grievances: too much government, too much taxation, too much product liability. Here was a World War II vet who had been in the middle of that God-awful battle in Italy. And here was a man, raised during the Depression, who had built a successful company that manufactured…what did he call it…a whole tree chipper, a Total Chiparvestor. And now Norval Morey had a plan to save America from its dependence on oil and it could go into effect right away.

"That's what I call one heck of plan," Reagan said to himself, cocking his head as he said it. That's also why he had written two scripts and would be doing two broadcasts on Morey's wood energy theme. He entitled them, Wood I and Wood II.

"Whenever you're ready, governor," O'Connor said, showing three fingers, then dropping them one at a time before punching in the tape and pointing at Reagan that he was on. The young lady looked at her version of the script to follow along as Reagan began his broadcast.

A s the decade of the 1970s progressed, Norval Morey now focused on two agendas, both crystal clear in his mind, and sometimes they complemented each other. One was the conversion of woody biomass into electricity. The other was a political reformation that called for less government regulation, taxation and intrusion, which would create a more favorable business climate and keep the American dream alive. The national politician that Norval supported to lead the overhaul was the former governor of

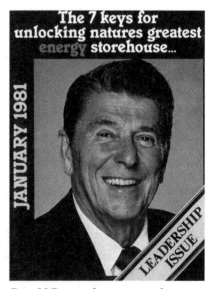

Ronald Reagan became a spokesperson for Norval Morey.

California, Ronald Reagan, and the amazing thing was that Reagan became a spokesperson for Norval's wood-to-electricity agenda two years before becoming president of the United States.

Norval usually had his nose to the grindstone at Morbark, especially when it was a fledgling company, but that's not to say Norval didn't harbor political opinions. In fact he had very strong ones, and they were consistent with those of many other combat veterans of World War II. The threat of Communism was very real to Norval, and to a lot of other people during the Cold War of the 1950s and 1960s. In the early 1960s Norval joined a chapter of the John Birch Society, which was an organization founded only several years earlier to contest Communism, Socialism and any other collectivist and potential New World order government, which Birchers felt were infiltrating into the United States and supported by sympathizers in the United States for the purpose of destroying the U.S. Constitution and the individual liberties guaranteed therein.

In the early 1960s Norval introduced his newest salesman, Larry Burkholder, to the John Birch Society. Burkholder joined it as well through the chapter in nearby Alma and went to the occasional meeting with Norval and his brother Ralph. Burkholder recalled that as conservative or politically to the right the John Birch Society may have been, other groups stepped even further "out there." One of them was the American Nazi Party.

Burkholder recalled when he and Norval were flying back to Detroit and Burkholder sat next to a dark-haired man with a mustache and rather dark piercing eyes. After a while they struck up a conversation and the man asked Larry if he followed politics. Larry said yes, and the man asked him if he was a conservative. Larry replied that he was "real conservative." "What's real conservative?" the man asked. "Well, I'm a member of the John Birch Society," Larry responded. The man smiled, "That's kind of elementary."

The man introduced himself as George Lincoln Rockwell and gave Larry his card, which said George Lincoln Rockwell was president of the American Nazi Party. Burkholder then recognized the name. Rockwell, who had served in the Navy, had founded the American Nazi Party in the late 1950s. He had been influenced by Senator Joseph

McCarthy's stance against Communism. Rockwell was now also known for promoting racial separation and denying that the Holocaust happened. Larry also recalled that somebody had tried to shoot Rockwell at the American Nazi Party headquarters in Arlington, Virginia.

When the plane landed in Detroit, Larry and Rockwell walked to the baggage claim as Rockwell smoked a corn cob pipe, a gesture of his admiration for General Douglas MacArthur. Norval caught up to them, met Rockwell and then Norval pulled Larry aside. "Get away from this guy," Norval said. "You don't want to be shot."

Later on Norval and Burkholder went to hear Rockwell speak, and not long after that, on August 25, 1967, Rockwell was shot and killed as he was pulling out of a laundromat at the Dominion Hills Shopping Center in Arlington.

Burkholder became enchanted with Reagan early on. Burkholder recalled being so impressed with a speech Reagan made in October 1964 on national television in support of Republican presidential candidate Barry Goldwater that Burkholder said to his family if Reagan ever pursued national politics he would actively support him.

At that time, Reagan was already known for his acting career, especially for his role as George "The Gipper" Gip in the movie "Knute Rockne, All-American." Before he became an actor, Reagan, who was born in Illinois and raised in Dixon, was a radio announcer, calling University of Iowa college football games and Chicago Cubs baseball games.

Reagan got a taste for politics when he served as president of the Screen Actors' Guild, during which he spoke out against fellow actors who were Communist sympathizers. He still considered himself a Democrat into the 1950s and into the 1960s, though endorsing Republican presidential candidates Dwight Eisenhower in 1952 and Richard Nixon in 1960. But in 1962 Reagan switched party allegiance to the Republicans, and while living in California he was urged by the Republican Party to run for governor of the state in 1966, which he did, and won, defeating two-term Democrat incumbent Pat Brown. By then Reagan stood tall for pro-business, lower taxes, limited government, anti-Communism and a strong military.

Ron Demlow grew up a half mile out from Winn, and knew all the Moreys growing up. The infamous one-room schoolhouse, Demlow School, where Norval had made a stab at education, was situated on Ron Demlow's grandfather's farm, thus the name.

"I knew Nub as long as I've known anybody," Demlow said.

Demlow, who would become a regional sales manager at Morbark, had an interest in local politics. He served for a time as Isabella County Treasurer.

Through political connections in 1968, Demlow came into possession of four tickets to a dinner/fundraiser for Richard M. Nixon, who had come out of hiding to run for president again, having lost a close presidential race to John Kennedy in 1960 and then losing the California governor's race to Pat Brown in 1962. Through the 1940s and 1950s Nixon had served in the House and Senate and as vice president under Dwight D. Eisenhower for two terms, but his political career had steered off course ever since.

Hosting the dinner was the man who had held the Grand Rapids congressional district seat in the U.S. House of Representatives since 1949. He was little known on the national scene, but Gerald Ford's day would come soon enough.

The keynote speaker was California Governor Ronald Reagan, who was gearing up to run for his second term and already receiving some encouragement to test the presidential waters.

Demlow thought Norval might enjoy the outing and invited him to go. The two old friends and their wives drove over to Grand Rapids for the event.

"Up on the podium that night was Ford, Nixon and Reagan," Demlow said. "We had no idea, of course, what the future would be for any of those three."

When Reagan started to speak, he seemed to be saying what Morey had been thinking for some time. Reagan pointed to the price of postage stamps. They had tripled in price to nine cents over the past few years. He then pointed to the price of a phone call from California to New York, which had gone from one dollar to 50 cents over the same period. The federal government was investigating Bell Telephone. Reagan's point was that the government-owned postal service price had tripled while the private enterprise price had been cut in half. "Who should be investigating who?" Reagan wanted to know.

The crowd, Demlow said, was electrified and Norval Morey was moved right along with the rest. The self-started businessman from the little potato farm in Winn was totally taken aback with this Reagan fellow.

"It was the kind of speech that just carries you along with it," Demlow said. "It just made such good, common sense. It just meant so much. From that night on, Norval was a big supporter of Reagan."

Demlow recalled: "You know, once Norval made up his mind about something, there was no changing it. He believed in free enterprise and in small government. He thought the best form of government was when it was as close to the people as possible. That's why he was such a big supporter of local politics."

Reagan's push for free enterprise and less government fell right into step with Norval's beliefs.

Reagan served two terms as governor, before deciding not to seek a third term and turning his eye on the presidency. Reagan ran against Gerald Ford for the Republican presidential nomination in 1976 and lost a close race, but Reagan touched a right wing conservative base, which felt Ford was too moderate. Ford, who was raised in Grand Rapids, had by then risen nationally in the House of Representatives to House Minority Leader, before assuming the position of Vice President, voted in by both houses of Congress after President Nixon's vice president, Spiro Agnew, was forced to resign in 1973 due to various criminal charges. When the Watergate scandal forced Nixon to resign in August 1974, Ford assumed the presidency, and then defeated Reagan for the party nomination, but lost to Georgia Governor and Democrat nominee Jimmy Carter, who had campaigned as a government outsider and a reformer following the scandals in the Nixon administration.

Just as Burkholder said he would, he strengthened his involvement in politics when Reagan ran against Ford. Norval was right behind him, not necessarily knocking on doors, but contributing money to the local district, the county, to Reagan directly and to the Republican National Committee and he would go to DC and do some fund raising.

Obviously Ford had a strong following in Michigan and in the immediate area, but Burkholder, with Norval's blessing, led a minor revolt of sorts within the county's Republican Party and endorsed Reagan over Ford. (The county overall was still heavy to the Democrats.) Norval grew even more involved as a member of the Republican Senatorial Trust, which was a fundraising arm of the party and through which Norval first conversed with Reagan as well as established senators such as Howard Baker from Tennessee, and newcomers such as John Heinz of Pennsylvania. The politicians referred to the man from Winn, Michigan as "the lumberjack."

Dennis Starner, who was a Congressional District Republican Chairman and a Reagan "worker bee," recalled, "I met Norval in early early Reagan. Norval was one of the early contributors. Norval was motivated because he was a rugged capitalist. He was like John Galt to a lot of folks. He was a free marketer. He later became a Republican Eagle, which was one of the top contributors to the Republican Party and Reagan. A lot of Morbark employees were involved locally in politics."

Starner said Norval did most of the talking during their conversations. "He was strongly opinionated. He would get upset with some of the problems he was having with the federal government, with getting steel for his company, tax issues and he would have some roaring lawsuits going on all the time."

Not far from home, Norval continued to back a local young Republican for a state seat in the Michigan House of Representatives. John Engler grew up on a cattle farm in Beal City, located near Mount Pleasant. Norval knew the family, including the father, Matt Engler, whom Norval had supported in an unsuccessful run for the Michigan House of Representatives in 1968.

The Engler family purchased calves from out west and fattened them on corn the family grew themselves. As a boy, John Engler and his six siblings were regular participants in the livestock competitions at the Isabella County Fair. Norval for many years purchased the annual winner of the competition at auction to help support the local 4-H clubs.

In 1970, as a 21-year-old senior at Michigan State University, Engler and a friend wrote a paper, which spelled out how a seat in the Michigan State House of Representatives could be won. The paper was intended to help none other than Isabella County Treasurer Ron Demlow get elected. When Demlow decided not to run, student Engler decided to throw his own hat into the ring.

"Norval knew me and I believe he thought I came from the right kind of background," Engler said. "I think he saw my participation in that race as pretty gutsy. He liked that I had the courage to run and I don't think he liked the incumbent. I guess he figured I couldn't do any worse a job for the district than what we were already getting."

Morey supported Engler financially in the race, which Engler won. Engler held the seat until 1978 and then ran for the Michigan State Senate and won again with Morey's financial help. Engler held the Senate seat to 1990, when he took his game to another level.

On the national landscape Norval was none too impressed with the new president, Jimmy Carter. "The growing national debt bothered Nub," Burkholder recalled. "Inflation, high interest rates, high unemployment, regulatory issues...Nub was very emotional and passionate in his concern over where the country was headed."

He did agree with Carter about one thing. In 1977, President Carter addressed the nation and called for less reliance on oil and more implementation of renewable energy sources, though Carter didn't specifically mention wood waste as one of those renewable energy sources.

Back in October 1973, as a protest to U.S. support of Israel during the Yom Kippur War, the Arab member countries of the Organization of Petroleum Exporting Countries (OPEC) plus Egypt and Syria proclaimed an oil embargo and production cut, resulting immediately in a seventy percent increase in the price of a barrel of oil to $5.11, which escalated even more to $12 per barrel in 1974. In the U.S. the retail price of a gallon of gasoline rose from 38 cents in May 1973 to 55 cents in June 1974. Some politicians called for a national gas rationing program. President Nixon requested that gasoline stations not sell gas on weekends, which resulted in long gas station lines during the week. The political upheaval was eventually resolved to some degree and oil prices mostly leveled off for a few years, but shell-shocked Americans now struck up a new conversation—energy independence.

Norval had for years been testing and promoting forest management thinning prescriptions in Northern hardwood woodlots that would gain additional wood products, enhance the value and health of the forest property, and most certainly include Morbark's whole tree chipper in his formula for forest success. When the oil crisis hit home, and with it the call for greater energy independence, Norval pounced on the concept of biomass power—the utilization of wood to create electricity for American society. While Norval believed in it for the good of mankind so to speak, he also recognized that it could become almost a failsafe market for the

Total Chiparvestor and possibly other Morbark products. Paper mills might still be experimenting with the implementation of whole tree chips, but the country needed wood chips for fuel now and forever.

Thus Norval pioneered the concept of using the waste wood in the nation's forests for energy. He called for the removal from the forests of dead, dying, diseased and overmature trees, as well as the undesirable species. This wood could be used to supply energy, while at the same time improving the timber stand and providing a better stock of trees to meet more

When Norval talked of wood energy, Morbark's whole tree chipper was always in the picture.

traditional needs such as paper and lumber.

On August 17, 1977, Norval spoke to a group of 17 members of the Michigan Legislature and laid out his plan. He pointed to the increase in the price of oil from $2.50 to $14 a barrel in recent years, and that the U.S. was importing nearly 50 percent of its oil and paying $40 billion a year out of the U.S.

"The Carter Administration has declared a 'moral war' on the energy crisis, but the government is scurrying around with programs of conservation…The Republicans say this is not the answer. We must find means of producing energy, not just saving it," Norval stated.

Norval chided those who believed the energy crisis was a smokescreen. "We look at it this way. Our heating bills are going up; our light bills are going up. The price of gasoline is going up. Everything else that is remotely tied to petroleum is going up. The government, the experts and the oil producers say the whole thing is due to the fact that our petroleum resources are dwindling and that someday, within our lifespan, we will run out of petroleum entirely! Whether that's true or not, we have taken their word for it and consider the situation serious.

"Maybe the era that saw this nation, in fact the whole world, be completely powered, industrialized and move from the automobile to the space age has just come to an end. Maybe the industrial giant that came to life with the age of petroleum will fall asleep as the petroleum resource dwindles and flickers out like a candle with its last desperate glow. What should we do? Sit and complain of the darkness?

"All my life I've heard about using solar energy. I've heard about wind energy. And they're still talking about it! People who seem to know say it will be another 20 to 30 years to develop any sort of impact with the so-called exotic energy resources. Nuclear energy generates as much controversy as it does energy. It seems easy to say, 'Let us go back to coal.' This is to say nothing of the environmental problems of cleaning up coal.

"Let us say this: what we propose should have been done whether we had an energy crisis or not. We say, 'Let's use the five billion tons of wood going to waste every year in this country.' We're not talking about the wood you make into lumber or furniture or any other commercial grade wood. We're talking about junk wood that litters our forests of this entire nation, wood that just rots and decays. There are five billion tons of it rotting every year. That's equal to more than eight billion barrels of oil in its energy equivalent when burned in boilers to make electricity. That amounts to three billion barrels more than this country uses annually at this time.

"If it makes sense to pick up the trash, to mow the lawn, to weed a garden, to collect garbage, then it makes sense to clean up the forests and utilize one of the greatest natural resources we have! It even makes more sense when you can solve the energy crisis at the same time.

"Remember, this isn't like solar energy or wind energy. It's here right now; we don't need to wait 20 years or even one year. The equipment, the technology and the resources are ready to start right today!"

It was a profound speech. Bill Nelson, who worked in advertising and marketing for Morbark, wrote most of Norval's speeches and columns that dealt with wood-to-energy. Nelson would talk to Norval, take notes and write the paper. Norval, however, never looked down at his written speech or notes while giving a talk. He always addressed the audience straight-on and spoke passionately. He often said it was like telling a story that you believed in.

Indeed Norval spearheaded an aggressive campaign for the conversion of woody biomass into energy that went on for years. And Norval got Ronald Reagan, who was on a fast track to becoming known as The Great Communicator, to disseminate Norval's message to America at-large.

It was no secret following his loss to Ford in the Republican Primary in 1976 that Reagan was gearing up for a more serious presidential run in 1980. In 1975 Reagan had started delivering syndicated radio broadcasts over hundreds of stations nationwide. His frustration at how the media scrambled the true intentions of the Republican Party and of Reagan himself had prompted Reagan to seek an outlet of direct communication. What better platform for a former radio man, with a strong voice and a clear conservative message, than the radio. His broadcasts hit home to millions of Americans who were struggling with high unemployment, skyrocketing interests, and a growing international perception that America was weak. From 1975 through most of 1979, Reagan delivered more than 1,000 broadcasts. Many historians credit these broadcasts as the driving force behind Reagan's victory over Carter in 1980. Two of those broadcasts were about Norval Morey's quest for wood-to-energy independence in America.

By this time, Norval was fully vested in Reagan, as was Morbark sales manager Burkholder, who had become chairman of the Isabella County Republican Party. Once viewed as renegades by the county's Republican Party, they now led the way. One of their causes and victories during this same period was a proposal to amend the state constitution known as the Headlee Amendment. The amendment put spending limits on state and local government by incorporating several provisions in favor of the average citizens: the state's total revenue could not exceed 9.49 percent of personal income in Michigan; if the state mandated that local governments provide new or expanded programs, the state had to provide full funding; local governments couldn't add new taxes or increase existing ones, or increase certain bonded indebtedness, without securing approval of the voters; and the state couldn't reduce the portion of its outlays that goes to local governments below the existing level of 41.61 percent. Norval liked the amendment because the state government was growing faster than the state's population, personal income and inflation. It was piling unfunded mandates upon local government, which in turn burdened taxpayers with even higher taxes and debt.

Norval was for it, but the man who organized and led it was Dick Headlee, the very same Dick Headlee who had served under Norval at Morbark and tried to undermine Norval's authority. The conflict had resulted in Headlee's departure from Morbark at Norval's direction. Headlee proceeded to become president and CEO of Alexander Hamilton Life Insurance, which under Headlee's leadership went from a domestic company with $100 million in assets to an international operation with $8 billion in assets. Headlee, who had previous political experience working with Governor George Romney, had many influential contacts, including Norval Morey, who had always admired Headlee's intelligence despite their run-in. Norval took the high ground and didn't harbor resentment for Headlee. He not only supported the Headlee Amendment, but he personally introduced Headlee at various functions and spoke on Headlee's behalf. Michigan voters passed the amendment in the general election of November 1978.

November 1978 was a good month for Norval. Early that month Norval contacted Reagan and asked to meet him at Reagan's office in Chicago. Norval was impressed by Reagan's "grasp and knowledge of the forest resource combined with his level headed approach to utilization of forest thinnings for energy." Apparently Norval impressed Reagan as well. Reagan, taking notes as he talked with Norval, wrote two scripts for his radio show. He recorded both of them later that month. The broadcasts actually aired in December to perhaps 30 million listeners. Reagan always opened his broadcasts with a teaser line before going to a commercial.

Wood I

Are you ready to learn that we really haven't been able to see the forest for the trees? I'll be right back.

When we have an opportunity to go to the ranch, which is not as often as we'd like, we're off and running. And once there we never have to ask, "what will we do?" There is an ongoing perpetual chore we can always turn to after a horseback ride or before for that matter.

Our house is heated only by fireplaces so the chainsaws are always gassed up and waiting. But they are used for more than building up the wood pile. Much of the ranch is covered by a beautiful forest of California. Live oaks and madrone trees. It's beautiful to look at but not easy to walk or ride through and I guess that's true of most woodland in America. You really can't see the forest for the trees.

Nancy and I and our friend Barney have taken to clearing pathways and even entire groves with two chainsaws, a pruning saw, and jeep and trailer. Our beautiful forest is a jungle of underbrush, windfalls, dead trees and dead limbs on live trees. The sun can't get through to the forest floor so new young trees die.

We've concentrated on one grove near the house. It is an arduous, back-breaking and slow job but the reward is great. The dead limbs and the prunings are piled high in the trailer and then hauled out to a clearing and stacked for burning when our California rainy season comes. The heavier limbs and fallen trees are cut to fireplace length and used to heat the house. Gradually this one grove has become park-like. The good trees can be seen, and the sun dapples the earth beneath as we walk or ride horseback through that particular grove. Already we've seen an increase in wildlife as deer browse on the new growth. Unfortunately there is no way we can ever complete the job on the entire forest and having it done would cost hundreds of dollars an acre.

Now what I've described is true of just about all the forest land in America. Whether we're talking commercial lumber land, privately owned timber or national forest, if there isn't a trail you can't go very far into the woods. But what if I told you forest land, which covers half the country—not counting groves of noncommercial lumber like ours, cannot only become beautiful and park-life with increased wildlife but it can do a lot to solve our energy problem?

No—I'm not suggesting we cut down our forests. Quite the contrary. Even the most ardent environmentalists approve the idea of clearing forests of dead wood and fallen limbs which make forest fires more probable and also more uncontrollable.

For some time now a gentleman named Norval Morey has been pleading the cause of harvesting junk wood as an energy source. He is president of Morbark Industries Inc. in Winn, Michigan. He explains that junk wood consists of trees in our forests that are dead, dying, diseased, overcrowded and overmature. He not only pleads the cause, he's doing something practical about it. Don't miss our exciting next installment with its amazing figures on a perpetual energy source and how easily it can be ours.

This is Ronald Reagan. Thanks for listening.

Wood II

On the preceding broadcast, I said there was an energy source close at hand, and inexhaustible. It's also more economical than oil, gas or coal. I'll be right back.

On the last commentary I referred to the president of Morbark Industries Inc. of Winn, Michigan, Norval Morey, who has been trying to make Washington aware of a self perpetuating energy source close at hand and greater than our entire import of oil from the OPEC nations.

In the U.S. (not including Alaska) we harvest about 1% of our wood per year for lumber and paper. Our forest lands produce each year 6 to 7 billion tons of new fiber. This means about 5 billion tons of the fiber is wasted each year as trees die or become old and cease to increase in size. Limbs falls, disease and rot set in. Young trees are stunted, unable to grow because they are smothered by windfalls or are unable to get needed sunlight. This 5 billions tons of waste wood is the equivalent of 8 1/2 billion barrels of oil. We only import 3 1/2 billion barrels a year.

What Mr. Morey is pointing out is that less than half of the waste or junk wood in our forests (which makes for a giant forest fire danger) can be used instead to produce steam or electricity equal to what we produce with the oil we import. And the forests will be healthier and more attractive.

Anticipating a question as to how we harvest this tangle of underbrush, dead trees, stunted trees and old trees, the answer is Morbark Industries is doing this every day. We all have some idea of regular harvesting practices, the chain saws, bulldozers, cable skidders and the debris left behind; tops, limbs, etc. This conventional method produces some 3 to 10 tons of wood per man/day. Morbark produces 50 tons per man/day of uniform size wood chips ready for the pulp mill.

An hydraulic shear reaches out and cuts the diseased or overage tree like you snip a cutting from a rose bush with a pair of clippers. A grapple pulls the tree and feeds it, limbs, top and all into a chiparvester. The chiparvestor is a machine that chews up the tree and spits it into a waiting truck in the form of wood chips and the truck heads for the power plant, factory or paper mill.

Morbark is already delivering to paper mills 2 grades of chips. One, the top grade is used to make the paper and the lower grade fuels the boilers.

There has been a recent addition to this mechanical chain—a gasifier which turns the waste wood into a natural gas increasing its heat energy. One fellow put it this way—"it even burns up the smoke." Incidentally whether burned as chips or gas, wood fiber is free of the pollutants found in other fuels. And when the machines pull out they leave a park-life forest behind with new shoots sprouting from the root systems, providing feed for wildlife.

The terms used to describe the process is environmental thinning and we have in the U.S. 736 million acres designated as commercial grade forests. We don't know how many millions of acres of groves and timber in addition. But in that commercial forest land there is an estimated 100 billion tons of trees of which 40% is junk or waste wood and the supply renews itself on a permanent basis.

This is Ronald Reagan. Thanks for listening.

Norval, with wife Jeri at center, was one of Reagan's earlier big-time supporters.

Norval, Burkholder and Morbark quickly took advantage of the greatest sales pitch ever made, and distributed Reagan's broadcast accompanied by a video of an "Environmental Thinning" operation. In fact they produced and distributed volumes and volumes of literature and data, some of it quite remarkable, to support their push for wood energy, much of it based on field work with the U.S. Forest Service. They also came up with "buzz words" such as "Environmental Thinning," as Reagan had referenced in his broadcast. In one of their publications they defined it as "a process of selectively taking out diseased, dead, overmature and overcrowded trees. It utilizes the entire tree and leaves the forest in an environmentally enhanced condition." Morbark said it employed three basic pieces of equipment— the feller-buncher shear, the grapple skidder and the whole tree chipper or Total Chiparvestor. In addition to producing high grade chips for paper production, environmental thinning emphasized fuel chips for energy, not only for electricity on the public grid, but for forest products mills to burn and produce their own energy to meet their own high energy requirements.

A Morbark publication stated, "If you pay $8.50 a ton for energy wood, the mill can run the chips over a (Morbark) Class-a-Fiber screen and separate out the grade chips for paper. This has proven to yield 50 to 60 percent high quality chips. A cost of $1.00 per ton for screening results in the true cost of approximately $10 per ton for high grade chips. If the mill desires to credit $15 per ton to high grade chips and $5.00 per ton to energy wood (the prerogative of the mill), in actuality they would be getting their energy wood free." The publication also emphasized that under new pending legislation, such energy efficient mills could qualify for special benefits.

Based on its own field work, including its own forestry and company logging operations, in collaboration with the Forest Service, Morbark said the total forest biomass in the U.S. was more than 100 billion tons; and that five billion tons annually should be environmentally thinned to remove waste wood, which, in collaboration with an annual harvest for commercial use products and accelerated growth brought on by the environmental thinning along with new planting, would maintain a constant inventory of 90-95 billion tons of fiber throughout the nation's forests.

Another buzzword was Biotherm Energy, which is what they called the wood energy concept, and which also became the name of a company they formed that introduced a gasification burner which was installed at the Morbark plant. Norval said an entire new stream of small (biomass power) electricity plants producing 10-20 megawatt was the most feasible scenario for a true alteration of the electricity generating infrastructure in America. He cited Michigan as an example where the state's forestlands could support as many as 300 plants of 20 megawatt capacity, each plant costing $5 million to construct. Each plant would employ 25-30 persons,

Norval and his team at Morbark flooded the market with wood-to-energy developments.

but also directly enhance the labor market associated with getting wood to the plant. Locating smaller power plants nearer the forested areas would diminish wood production and transportation costs.

Norval liked this concept of smaller, decentralized power plants, especially for cogeneration, where the plant could re-use its thermal energy for heating, rather than waste it, while selling excess electricity into the power grid. Another term for this was distributed generation, which was believed to be more efficient and cost-effective with regard to the transmission of power because it minimized congestion of power during peak times, and also offered environmental friendliness compared to air emissions issues with large, centralized power plants.

Norval also liked this concept of decentralized power from a security standpoint. Larry Burkholder recalled when they were in New York City for a meeting and looking out over the city from their hotel room. "Norval said, "You don't realize what would happen if somebody blew up a nuclear reactor or oil refineries. Can you imagine New York City blacked out? Everything shut down. People crowding into the streets and practically standing on top of each other. No food. No law. I've been in situations where there's no law and people are desperate. You don't want to go there!"

Burkholder, somewhat puzzled, asked, "Who would want to blow up something like that?"

Norval replied, "Terrorists."

It was the first time Burkholder had heard the word used in such a context.

Morbark's Biotherm Gasifier would be an ideal installation for such plants, Norval hoped. It was described as a device that swirled the wood into a vortex formed by powerful jet streams of air. Intense friction created wood gas with high BTU potential. This gas would serve as highly efficient fuel for firing industrial boilers.

In another one of Norval's numbers scenarios, he estimated that the cost of gas fuel in 1978 was $2 per million British Thermal Units (BTU's) and that oil would cost $2.45 per million BTU. Biotherm Energy, however, would cost $1.20 per million BTU's or less than half the cost of oil. Furthermore, recent statistics indicated that the cost of oil and gas would each rise at an average annual increase of 10 percent per year to $4.72 per million BTU's by 1987 for gas and to $5.78 for oil. Wood costs would go up, but the annual increase would be only half that rate or 5 percent. So that even by 1987 wood would only cost $2.72 per million BTU's.

All of this wood energy noise Norval was making resounded all the way to the nation's most prestigious higher institution of learning, Harvard University in Cambridge, Massachusetts. The Harvard Business School invited Norval to speak before it students, faculty and business executive guests in order to enlighten them on his wood-to-energy plan. Larry Burkholder and a couple of others from Morbark accompanied Norval.

Burkholder recalled, "They took us in and they had this fish bowl set-up with Norval standing down at the podium and speaking up to the students sitting up above with their legal pads and pencils. He was

The man with the sixth grade education caused the Harvard Business School to stand and take notice.

supposed to talk for an hour but he talked for two and a half hours. They were fascinated. He was a motivational guy. He was very believable, very humble but very sure of himself, kind of like a Will Rogers."

Norval, dressed in a nice suit, didn't glance at his notes or use any graphics. He looked up and around at his audience, and started out, "I'd like to tell you a story."

Norval went through the evolvement of wood-to-energy, noting that it had a long history, but its revival had come, whether to generate electricity for the public, steam for industrial processes, or provide heating for institutions such as colleges, hospitals and prisons. He pointed to four reasons why: 1) The ongoing oil and gas crisis; 2) The greatly improved wood extraction technologies in the forests, including the Total Chiparvestor; 3) The greater realization of the product potential in whole tree production beyond conventional building products; 4) Increasing research and supporting data on the inventory and benefits of forest biomass for energy as compared to traditional fossil fuels such as coal.

Norval said that by demonstrating the economic feasibility of electricity from wood, he hoped to persuade state and federal authorities to back the idea on a large scale. Incentives might take the form of tax advantages or lower interest rates on borrowings, or subsidization of research and development costs, as well as education resources diverted to the development of trained engineers and wood power station operatives.

Norval concluded that he felt once again in his life he seemed to be ahead of his contemporaries, but that finally after three years of campaigning as to the merits of biomass energy, some recognition (for his concept) had been forthcoming.

The students responded with numerous questions before rising to give Norval a standing ovation. Here was the farm boy who couldn't read very well, who didn't finish seventh grade, receiving great admiration from the best young minds in America because of his commitment and plan to fix America's energy problem. It was truly an Horatio Alger story.

Not long after the Harvard speech, Norval spearheaded the formation of the National Wood Energy Association, with Larry Burkholder as its president. The goal of NWEA was to alter the energy strategy of the

United States to include wood energy as a major alternative, supported by the readily available wood resource and existing technologies. The NWEA board included John Rumble from Clark Equipment Company, Dennis Vollmershausen of Eaton Corp. and Len Vizina of National Hydro-Ax. Burkholder joined Norval as a regular spokesman for wood-to-energy, and Norval's nephew, Jerry Morey, also delivered numerous talks.

Indeed biomass power plants began springing up in the North and West as companies received legislated incentives, tax benefits and guaranteed power purchase contracts and rates for a number of years. Norval frequently traveled around the country to converse with these participants, especially about their feedstock procurement methods and technologies. He attended a number of ground breaking ceremonies for such facilities.

Oil prices hiked again in 1980 in the wake of the Iranian Revolution, which disrupted oil production and exports. Oil prices shot up to $38 per barrel. This development along with booming interest rates contributed to Reagan's victory over Carter for the presidency. Norval now had a friend in the highest of places.

Reagan wasn't the only politician speaking Norval's language. Senator Howard Baker of Tennessee said, "I know that it is the desire of the American people to be free of our present dependence on foreign fuel sources…To underemphasize or ignore this vital and abundant domestic fuel source, wood, is to ignore the wishes of the American people. That is something I do not wish to see happen." Senator John Durkin of New Hampshire stated, "A vast almost incalculable energy resource exists today—not in some foreign country or future world—but in the forests of the Northeast, Southeast, and Northwest."

Following Reagan's election, Morbark produced a series of special magazines called *The 7 Keys for unlocking nature's greatest energy storehouse.* The "7 keys" were Availability, Leadership, Forest Management, Technology, Economics, Education and Markets. A magazine was published for each of the seven themes. The Leadership issue, which was also called the Presidential Inaugural Issue, ran President Reagan's photo on the cover, and inside it ran photos and those quotations from senators Baker and Durkin, along with Senator Jesse Helms of North Carolina, Georgia Governor George Busbee, senators Bob Packwood and Mark Hatfield from Oregon, Senator John Melcher of Montana and Congressman Jim Weaver from Oregon.

Back at the factory Morbark wasn't sitting on its Total Chiparvestor laurels. It now added a new machine to its environmental thinning equation, a three-wheel feller-buncher for cutting down trees. In the late 1970s a group of American Pulpwood Association members toured South Africa and discovered the Bell tractor, a highly maneuverable three-wheel machine developed by Irvine Bell in the late 1960s. Some people in the APA group suggested that Bell investigate the machine's potential in the Southern United States, where the harvesting situation showed some similarities to that of South Africa. Bell sent a couple of representatives to the U.S., including Russ Stevenson, who visited Norval and the Morbark facility. Norval immediately took to the concept and visited the Bells in South Africa. Within months a joint venture, Mor-Bell Equipment, was formed. The first machine, the Mor-Bell Logger, actually wasn't a feller-buncher but a combination skidder and loader equipped with a telescoping slide-boom and a grapple, but Morbark soon put its shear attachment on it. The Mor-Bell was said to be twice as fast and much more nimble with the tightest of in-woods turning abilities compared to conventional feller-bunchers. After producing and selling several models of the three-wheeler, the partnership ultimately dissolved several years laters, as Morbark's service support and dealer pipeline probably wasn't as efficient as it should have been. But Morbark continued to manufacture its version of a three-wheeler, called the Wolverine, said to be sturdier and provide more comfortable features for the operator. Morbark had success with the machine until bowing out of the market in the late 1990s as the heyday of the three-wheeler ran its course.

Another successful new product that complemented Morbark's reputation for chipping expertise was the Eeger Beever, a portable machine for chipping brush, limbs and small trees. It featured a disc-style chipper with two half knives, special feedworks and operated with minimal fuel consumption. Norval credited Lee Smith with designing it and building

Morbark had some success with its three-wheel machine partnership.

the first one, but Norval felt it wasn't cost efficient. Later, when the recession of that period subsided, Norval said he sat down to redesign the brush chipper with his nephew Mike Morey, who was in charge of whole tree chipper and now brush chipper manufacturing, and Dave Forquer, who had worked at Morbark for 15 years in drafting and in the steel room. Norval explained that they used the one knife disc and feedworks and built up the rest of the machine.

Norval said he had Mike and Dave build two dozen of the machines, followed by additional improvements, and then set up a production line that could produce 100 machines a month. An early problem, Norval explained, was that the welds (the hub and knife holders were welded to the disc) had broken on a couple of machines in the field and to correct the problem they began bolting the hub to the disc and developed a new knife holder to bolt the knives into the machine. Norval felt they should change the machines in the field and said this cost the company a million dollars. But as it turned out, Norval recalled, it probably wasn't necessary as they later discovered that the problem was actually poor quality welding on a few machines.

Soon the great exodus began. Smith apparently resigned over issues not related to the brush chipper. Then Forquer and Mike Morey both resigned in early summer 1983. Mike, who was said to be a lot like Norval, said he was disagreeing more and more with Norval's insistence on certain design changes to the brush chipper and the whole tree chipper. Norval recalled that Mike told him that Mike and Forquer were going to build their own brush chipper from their own design. Their company was called Foremost Fabrications and the shop was only a short drive from the Morbark plant. Other Morbark employees apparently joined them. Forquer left the venture a short while later, as he and Mike had differences. Mike stayed the course.

"I think it stunned Nub when Mike left," Larry Burkholder recalled. "It stunned all of us. I think you had two strong personalities."

At first Norval doubted that Mike could make a go of it. But Mike did indeed establish a major competitor for Morbark. Mike would call his company Bandit Industries. Such competition, Norval said, caused Morbark to operate with "very little profit margin" in the Eeger Beever, which angered Norval because he felt Morbark was the company that had done all the upfront work on it. Norval also felt somewhat betrayed.

Norval's son, Lon, recalled that his dad fired back at Mike with two lawsuits, one for taking sensitive information and one for patent infringement, and that both cases were settled with Bandit paying Morbark. By then, Jerry Morey, also Norval's nephew, who had worked at Morbark for 24 years and risen in the ranks in sales management, had also resigned from Morbark and joined his cousin Mike at Bandit. Jerry recalled that the lawsuits were ongoing when he made the changeover. "We ended up settling it," he said. "We paid him (Norval) some money." Jerry said it was becoming increasingly stressful to work with Norval, especially in finalizing sales deals and product line promotion. Jerry joined Bandit to oversee sales, while Mike handled manufacturing. Norval was known to drive slowly past the Bandit plant now and then to gauge the activities.

Thirty years later, animosities still persisted over the departure of the nephews.

Through the years the creation of a competitor chipper manufacturing company by former Morbark employees became amazingly routine. In addition to Bandit Industries, former Morbark employees formed Trelan, Blue Ox, Dynamic Industries and Woodsman, which says a lot for the training and experience provided by Norval and Morbark, though the departures caused varying degrees of hardship.

"I never heard Nub wish any of them well and some of them he never held in the highest regards and some of them he just did not discuss," recalled Norval's son-in-law, Lucky Robison, who was promoted to plant manager when Mike Morey left. Robison joined Morbark in 1977 and had risen to a regional sales manager position when he became plant manager. "I'm sure Nub felt everyone had the right to try and do something better," Robison said.

Norval and Morbark continued to push wood conversion to electricity. Norval was instrumental in convincing Central Michigan University in nearby Mount Pleasant to convert from gas to a wood-fired power plant. Morbark won the bid to supply 44,000 green tons of whole tree chips and wood fiber on an annual basis, with the chips coming directly from Morbark's company chipping operation or its storage facility at Winn. About the same time Morbark guaranteed the fuel chips supply, through local whole tree chip suppliers and sawmills, for Thermo Electron's new wood fired power plant in Whitefield, New Hampshire. The plant was later sold to Whitefield Power and Light Company.

But almost as soon as those many biomass power plants started operation in California and in the Northern U.S., oil and gas prices leveled off, and even declined and would remain recessed all the way until the turn of the century. However, more wood products plants continued to include cogeneration with wood as one of their options, along with gas, for powering and heating their plants, which meant Morbark's whole tree chipper business still had a reliable market for fuel chips in addition to clean chips for certain types of paper manufacturing.

Norval wouldn't live to see it, but when oil prices exploded to $100 a barrel in 2011, a rejuvenation occurred in woody biomass to electricity. The federal government and many state governments got behind it with significant subsidization and lending. Not only were new woody biomass power plants built, but some existing coal-fired plants converted to wood as their fuel source. What Norval hadn't seen was the number of large industrial wood pellet plants that would be built and started up in the Southern U.S., relying heavily on wood chips as their raw material to produce wood pellets for export to Europe, which was abandoning fossil fuels in favor of renewable energy. All of this activity was based on what Norval had preached four decades earlier, that the U.S. forests possessed enough biomass and wood waste to support wood energy as a factor in America's energy infrastructure. Norval Morey was the father of modern wood energy.

Going into 1986 Morbark was reporting $30 million in annual sales from an offering of 30 products in forestry, sawmill and municipal markets. It employed more than 300 at its factory, which had grown to 700,000 square feet. It had just opened seven new company stores: Morbark California, Morbark Louisiana, Morbark Maine, Morbark Mississippi, Morbark North Carolina, Morbark Northwest, Morbark Wisconsin. But the best times were still ahead. Almost on cue, a new opportunity revealed itself that complemented Morbark's product offerings and maintained an energy twist. In 1986 Morbark introduced The Waste Recycler. The practice of hauling tree stumps to landfills was expensive and not practical for the landfills, and meanwhile new clean air legislation was cracking down on open burning of stumps and brush. The machine not only converted stumps into wood chips, mulch and top soil, but also processed tangled brush, pallets, ties, large timbers and old lumber.

"That was Nub's," recalled Gary Bardos. "He designed it. It had a big eight foot cutting wheel. There was nothing out there grinding stumps like that." Bardos, another of Norval's newphews, became an assistant to Robison in the plant. Bardos had been running Morbark's woods crew, which was still active as a contractor to deliver chips to various paper mills.

The 70,000 lb. Waste Recycler measured nearly 49 feet in length and 10 ft. in width and was powered by a 650 horsepower diesel engine. Basically a powered ram plate at one end of a trough moved toward and

Morbark continued to bring innovative technologies to the market, including the Waste Recycler and the Tub Grinder.

forced the stumps and debris into the large rotating chipper disc with spiral knives at the other end. The machine was labeled the Stump Disintegrator when Norval filed for the patent in August 1986. The patent was issued in 1988 and listed Norval and Ivor Bateman as the inventors. Norval compared it somewhat to the old Veg-O-Matic kitchen appliance.

As successful as The Waste Recycler was, Morbark's next product, the Tub Grinder, hit the jackpot. Bardos had seen a variation of one in operation and brought the idea back to the Winn plant. "It was a gold mine for us in the early 1990s," Bardos said. A loader placed stumps and brush into a 12 foot diameter tub where a 16 inch diameter hammermill with multiple fixed hammers powered by a 650 horsepower diesel engine broke down the material. The grinder could process up to a four foot diameter stump along with railroad ties, pallets and other waste in excess of one ton per minute. Morbark would manufacture several models and variations of the grinder. Norval gained yet another patent for the tub grinder in 1995.

The tub grinder, along with expansion of other existing product lines would dramatically lift Morbark's annual sales into the $100-120 million range in the early 1990s. The irony is that Norval wasn't a big believer in the tub grinder when he first saw it. In fact he said it was "the stupidest thing." Then he asked Burkholder how many they could sell. "Twenty this year, forty next year," Burkholder replied. Norval responded, "That's a lot of money."

The Waste Recycler, the Tub Grinder and various screening systems would be managed out of a new company, Recycling Systems Inc. It would be one of several companies that Morbark reorganized as separate subchapter S corporations for each product line beginning in 1988. Ron Poparello, who oversaw finances, recalled, "Product liability was a big consideration. The other consideration was Norval felt this would give a number of individuals the opportunity to be involved with running a company and owning a small amount of stock in it. I know that he believed that if people had a personal interest in the ownership they would work more effectively than if they were just making salaries."

Larry Noch, who started at Morbark in 1984 as a credit manager and would succeed Poparello as head of finance, said the number of different corporations increased to more than two dozen. "Norval would call me in and say set up a company and put this guy in charge and call it this," Noch recalled. "Even though Norval was the main shareholder, the people he put in charge had never owned anything in their lives and now they had a piece of the action and they were proud of that."

Norval's son-in-law Lucky Robison, who was moved from plant manager to president of one of the newly formed companies, Chiparvestor Inc., thought another reason for the reorganization was that Norval wanted to start training others to take over when he backed away.

Some of the earlier companies included Recycling Systems, Inc.; Chiparvestor, Inc.; Wolverine Equipment Corp.; Morbark Sawmill Supply; Beevers Inc.; E-Z Chippers, Inc.; Flails, Inc.; Sharp Edge, Inc. Morbark Industries continued to handle central purchasing, parts and accounting. Morbark Forestry Machine & Shop Division fabricated its knuckleboom loaders as well as internal components that were purchased by the other affiliates. "By all of them buying out of that company, they've been able to buy the tools and machinery to produce it cheaper than we could get it done outside," Norval said. The sales and marketing efforts were channeled into a separate company as well, Morbark Sales Corp. At this same time the company was rebuilding its dealer network especially for the after sales support, which the company's direct marketing approach through its dozen or so Morbark stores didn't always adequately address, especially as the volume of business escalated. Norval started what became known as Demo Days at the Morbark plant, an annual gathering of dealers and customers for viewing live demonstrations of the Morbark product line.

Right behind the tub grinder came two more major product developments. In 1991 Morbark introduced the combination Flail/Chiparvestor, which included rotary chain flail drums for removing bark and limbs prior to the log entering the chipper. The point of the machine was to make good enough quality chips for paper manufacturing. Various flail drum systems had been used for many years, but Morbark promoted its machine as an improvement in handling multiple small diameter logs fed in side by side as well as improved debarking efficiency and more user-friendliness with regard to the maintenance and replacement of the flail drum parts. This patent wasn't filed until May 1993 and was issued in June 1994, listing Norval and Milan Robison as the inventors.

Another patent for Norval during this period was the Drum-Type Wood Chipper. Bardos recalled, "He said 'we're not going to build that disc chipper anymore. We're all drum.' I'm thinking we just gave up 50 percent of the market share. But in the end he was right; everybody moved to drum."

The knock on the disc-type chipper, which Morbark and others had been using, was that feed rates were significantly lower, causing some inconsistency in the operation of the chipping knives, leading to collision of chips behind the disc and in the discharge chute, generally slowing chips movement and discharge. Accordingly, the disc had to be rotated faster than necessary to chip the wood to ensure that the chips were properly discharged. The drum-type chipper, an older style than the disc, operated with equally spaced knives on a certain size of diameter drum. But it required blowers or augers to release the chips from the knives and to propel the chips through the chute, and thus engines with large horepowers were required. Still, drum chippers would stall. And the engines often required expensive emissions control equipment.

Norval proposed building spacing or openings around the knives for the cut wood chips to move through and into pockets behind the knives, remaining there until the drum rotated to the dischage chute, at which point under centrifugal force the chips were expelled from the pockets, through the openings and into the discharge chute. By maintaining the momentum of the chips, this new chipper could operate with a smaller power source than previous drum-style or disc-style chippers.

In 1990 and 1991 Morbark invested $1.6 million to install four computerized lathes and machining centers. In the first quarter of 1993 Morbark completed its third major plant expansion in as many years, adding 400,000 square feet on top of the 100,000 square feet added in each of 1990 and 1991, at a combined cost of $7 million, bringing the Morbark facility up to 1.3 million square feet. The newest building

Norval understood the full potential of the forest if it was managed properly.

housed 10 new assembly lines, each 480 feet long. Another new product to be built on those lines was a knuckleboom loader as Morbark entered the loader market with the Model 1000B.

This was an amazing stretch of technological developments and company sales growth that Norval spearheaded at Morbark. His son-in-law, Robison, commented, "To know Norval and watch him orchestrate the operation of Morbark was to respect a man that would live and die by his decisions."

Noch recalled, "It was Norval's company and Norval ran it. He put a lot of faith into the people who worked for him so you weren't looking over your shoulder all the time, but when he found something he was interested in, he told you how to do it and expected you do it that way."

His son, Lon, who headed the parts departments for years at Morbark before adding human resources to his responsibilities, commented, "He was such a true visionary and a realist; you had a hard time arguing with him. Everything had to be his way. He had the right to have it his way. He didn't have a lot of patience with people sometimes. I think because he had such a strong common sense approach that he couldn't understand why other people didn't see it his way. But he was so far ahead of everyone else in his thinking."

Of course the more products Norval and Morbark put into the marketplace, the more exposed the company became to the encroachment of product liability. The irony was that the equipment Morbark manufactured made working conditions much safer compared to earlier years when woods operations were so heavy to manual labor.

Noch was heavily involved in preparing Morbark's product liability cases, most of which involved personal injury or death, though not always. "Norval hated lawyers with a passion," Noch said. "He saw no value whatsoever in what they did or the kind of advice they would try and give him. Norval's position on lawsuits was that 99.9 percent of all accidents were user error; that the people using the product got over-confident and complacent around the machinery because they were there every day, were used to the danger and would take shortcuts. We would investigate all of the accidents and Norval would look at it and say basically it's not our fault, so defend it, we're going to trial, we didn't do anything wrong, no settlement, end of story, go."

The key to the Morbark defense was Norval himself. He served as Morbark's expert witness. "Whether it was a deposition or in trial he was a master of directing the conversation," Noch said. "Somebody would ask him a question and he would talk about what he wanted to talk about. It might be on point, might not. The plaintiff's lawyer had an awful time trying to corner him."

Norval was at his best when testifying before a jury. Cases took the Morbark team all over the country, but Norval only brought a duffel bag with him and one suit, and whether the trial lasted one day or five, he wore the same suit to court. He would look right at the jury and tell a story, the story of Norval Morey, how he grew up, what he had over-come, how he made something out of his life. The jurors took to him.

Noch recalled a case that took them to court in a small town out-side of Dallas. The plaintiff had purchased a tub grinder from Morbark for processing and reducing the volume of waste he was accumulating at a condemned housing demolition project for the city. Morbark had run advertisements that the tub grinder could reduce the volume of such material seven-to-one, which meant tremendous cost savings for contractors hauling dumpsters of this waste to a landfill. Noch said after the Texas contractor would knock down a house, he kept running a bulldozer over the debris, squashing the material flatter and flatter to the ground, then scraping it up and loading the dumpsters. His lawsuit against Morbark claimed the tub grinder wasn't living up to its seven-to-one reduction billing, that he was getting more like four-to-one. He wanted a payment from Morbark for the difference.

"Norval's not paying him a dime," Noch recalled. "Norval says that machine is doing what it's supposed to be doing. You can get seven-to-one reduction, four-to-one, ten-to-one, it all depends. So it goes to trial. Norval gets on the stand and gets to tell his story. Here's who I am, here's what I've done and the jury is eating that up; they love him to death. It's just Norval telling them his story and telling them why he built that piece of equipment the way he did. He's the inventor of the machine. And here's this other guy telling them how he's been wronged."

The jury took an hour and a half and decided against the Texas contractor. "Then the jurors came out and wanted to meet Norval and shake his hand," Noch said. "Even jurors who held his fate in their hands endeared to his story of trying to do the right things and being a hard working regular kind of guy. This was not uncommon when Norval testified."

Noch said Morbark achieved a tremendously high success rate in product liability cases. The worst verdict could have been much worse. A contractor in White Cloud, New York had kicked at a log stuck in a brush chipper and lost his leg below the knee. The trial jury awarded the man $13 million, of which Morbark was responsible for 25 percent. Morbark appealed and the ruling was overturned. It went back for retrial, which resulted in a hung jury. Headed to a third trial, the parties agreed to a settlement of $100,000. "That's success when you can defend your way through it," Noch said.

In and out of the courtroom, Norval and his company had experienced unprecedented growth in the 1980s and into the 1990s. He rewarded his employees accordingly. In addition to setting up a system of separate companies that gave ownership shares to loyal managers, and establishing a 401k for all employees, Norval provided money gifts to his key employees as well. In 1991 he gifted a total of $3 million and in 1995 another $5 million. Each time he gave an employee anywhere from $3,000 to the maximum annual tax-exempt amount allowed by law of $10,000. He did this in the form of a term interest bearing note that the company actually owed Norval. He gifted them to the employees and when the notes became due, the company paid them to the employees over a 10 year period. The payment included the principal and the accrued interest earned while being open. For the most part the notes became due when a person reached 55. Norval did this with family members, too.

"Norval really didn't like the fact that the government kept changing the retirement age," Noch said. "He figured the government had made a deal with people and forced them to put money into this thing and now they kept making it harder and harder for them to get it."

In his letters to his employees informing them of their gifts, Norval said, "You should be able to decide when you want to retire, not the government, therefore I'm giving you this gift that is a note that will come due when you're around 55. It's going to sit and earn money as a note to the company until then. It'll pay you this much interest each month and if all goes well this is what you'll have when you're 55. I want you to take that money and consider it my way of letting you determine when you want to retire."

It was like they would receive social security ahead of getting their real social security," Noch said. "Norval did these things, and it worked fine."

Noch explained that Norval didn't have an expansive portfolio of stocks and bonds and various investments, but invested most everything he made back into the company to make it bigger. So when he gifted away that money, such as to the employees, this money was debt that the company owed him, and which the company now owed the employees; all the while making sure the IRS wouldn't be able to get its teeth into it.

One new addition to the employment roster in 1989 was Dan Brandon. Norval needed a new set of eyes and ears so to speak, and a new voice for the growing business of Morbark. Brandon, a journalist by trade who was from Lansing, became the marketing and communications director, reporting directly to Norval.

Brandon's job interview with Norval lasted four hours. Typical of Norval's interviews, they didn't talk about the actual job, but more about people in general and politics. Toward the end of it, Norval noticed Brandon had brought along a leather portfolio, which contained samples of Brandon's work. "I see you have some stuff with you," Norval said. Then he gestured it away with his hand. "I wouldn't be able to judge whether it's any good or not. I don't need to see it."

Also not unusual in Norval's hiring process—after Norval offered Brandon the position and some time later when Brandon reported for his first day of work—nobody had ever heard of him because Norval hadn't told anybody about the new hire. A personnel lady quickly went to talk to Norval who confirmed the hire.

Norval and Morbark needed Brandon's communications talents especially as the company expanded into new recycling and grinder product lines. It quickly became apparent to Brandon that his new boss was someone special. "He struggled with reading, but he was good with numbers and the mechanical side of life," Brandon said. "He was always adventurous with R and D, always trying to find the next great idea. He was the R and D. I can remember him sitting at his desk and drawing things up with a pencil and ruler. He was brilliant. He was a real unique man."

Brandon also immediately saw that his new company was totally unconventional compared to other corporations he had done some work for.

"The family was completely intertwined with the company. Norval gave any relative a job that wanted a job, even it was just sweeping the floors. He really believed in the small town, rural, hardworking, hard scrabble kind of families that are still in that area. He always identified with that. He was always proud of how many people he employed; the more he could expand and the more people he could employ the better."

Sitting in on his first planning meetings, Brandon saw Norval at his best. "The man had presence. He had that deep baritone voice and he commanded a room and he didn't need to raise his voice to get his points across. He might occasionally put his fist on the table. Often there would be long discussions, opinions on the table, and at the end he would say this is what we're going to do. He was a dictator but he did value other people's opinions and didn't want to be surrounded by yes men."

Brandon also soon encountered the classic internal phone call from Norval, which could send people scattering into hiding. "When someone called you internally the number lit up on your phone. He was number 100. When that lit up your heart took a little skip. You would answer the phone and he would always say the same thing: 'Have you got a minute?' Now how do you answer that?"

Brandon soon came up with his own standard and safe response: "Yeah, I've got a minute for you."

Often Norval would call Brandon in and say he wanted to do some ads and he would show Brandon some photos and where he wanted to crop them with yellow post-its. "He had a sense of what he wanted, but he didn't exactly know how to say it," Brandon recalled. "When I would write something for him, he would have me come in and sit down and read it to him, because he got a better sense of the flow of the words that way, rather than trying to struggle to read it himself."

As good a run as Norval's company was having, Norval was on a roll politically as well, putting a lot of money and time in support of Reagan, who served two terms as president, and doing likewise for John Engler, who after nearly three decades as a representative and senator in the Michigan state government, was elected governor in 1990.

After serving in the Michigan state house and senate since 1970, with Norval backing him all the way, Engler joined the race for governor, this time with his sights set on defeating sitting governor, James Blanchard. Morey's support never waivered. While Engler can't recall the exact amount Norval contributed, he does recall it was substantial. "Norval would not only write me a check from him, he would then turn around and raise money for me from among his friends and other people," Engler said. "I think he raised a lot right there at Morbark."

Again, Engler unseated an incumbent. "In all, I ran in 10 elections—four of the races were against incumbents and in three of those I was the underdog—and Norval helped me each time and I won each time." Through it all, Engler stood for privatization of services, tax reduction, educational reform and welfare reform.

Engler saw Norval Morey as a trusted friend who never minced words but also as a visionary genius who foresaw the future of wood biofuels before anyone else. "People who underestimated Norval based on how he came across were very mistaken," Engler said. "His genius in so many areas surprised plenty of people through the years, but he was never one to try and impress people. He didn't care what anyone thought about him or didn't seem to care. I think he was totally at ease with who he was and what he had accomplished. Like I said, he was a visionary. Just a brilliant guy."

Engler recalled with a laugh how Norval liked to implement a new idea. "If he wanted to expand the plant, he would just pace it off and start building," Engler said. "He wasn't going to wait around for architects or plans or permits. He just stepped off the new addition and said, 'All right, fellows, let's get going on this.' I just loved that about him."

In 2012 Engler served as executive director of the Business Roundtable, an association of CEO's based in Washington, D.C. "There was only one Norval Morey," Engler said. "He wasn't polished. He was direct. A straighter talker there never was. I will always owe him a debt of gratitude." Engler served three terms as governor during 1991-2003.

As for Ron Demlow, the man Engler replaced as a state representative candidate way back when, Engler would appoint him to the Michigan Forest Finance Authority, which was created to issue certain revenue obligations to be paid for with revenues from the sale of timber, provide for the acquisition of standing timber and timber cutting rights, and provide for certain forest management operations and practices.

Norval didn't back a winner every time, but he made a special acquaintance in Larry Reed, who lost a race as a Republican candidate for the U.S. Congress in Michigan's 10th district.

Reed was from Beaver Falls, Pennsylvania and earned bachelor's and master's degrees at colleges in Pennsylvania, after which he moved to Michigan to teach economics at Northwood University in Midland. During his stay there, Reed ran for the U.S. Congress in 1982. He knew Norval by reputation, especially for Norval's involvement in the Reagan campaign in 1980, and then met the man. They spoke a similar language.

"Norval had a deep seated concern about the size and intrusiveness of government," Reed recalled. "He saw it first hand in the regulations he had to deal with as a businessman and the taxes he had to pay. You couldn't have a meeting with him without him talking about the concerns he had about how fast government was growing and the dumb things it was doing."

Norval was extremely helpful to Reed financially both in the primary and the general election. "I know he leaned on friends and relatives to give to me," Reed said. "There were a lot of good folks close to him that I started getting one thousand dollar checks from for the campaign."

Reed may have lost the election, but he wasn't forgotten. Several years later a handful of men with heavy ties to the insurance industry formed the Mackinac Center for Public Policy as a non-profit "free market think tank." Its primary purpose would be to conduct research and provide data toward the understanding and development of state and local policy for the purpose of enhancing the lives of Michigan citizens, with emphasis on economics and citizen quality of life. In late 1987 this initial board of directors hired Reed as the center's first president. Reed had moved to Idaho and had been directing a policy institute there since 1984. Reed would do amazing things at the Mackinac Center, which was headquartered in Midland. Under Reed's leadership, the center became the largest and most influential state-based think-tank in the country.

Reed suspected that Norval was one of the drivers behind the formation of the center as well as Reed's hiring. Norval came to Reed and the center's assistance early on. In late 1989 the center published a small book of one hundred pages entitled, *Michigan: An Agenda for the Nineties.* The book was meant for the public at large, and was designed to inform citizens as to where the state stood on various developments and policies, the problems that existed such as overspending and high taxes, and how to go about correcting them. It included a 20 point agenda for the next governor and legislature to enact. But operating with a limited budget, the center printed only a thousand copies. Norval liked the little book so much, however, that he approached Reed and asked how they could send out 50,000 copies around the state. Reed said it was a matter of funding, and that the book cost less than a dollar apiece to print. Norval promptly provided a $50,000 grant to the center. The center printed up the 50,000 copies and distributed them throughout the state, including to 17,000 business people on the Michigan Chamber of Commerce mailing list.

"That thing took off," Reed recalled. "It was cited in the media. It turned out to figure with some prominence in the 1990 gubernatorial campaign because it really laid out some negative things the current governor was doing and John Engler picked up on it. I remember John later saying that by the end of his first term he had enacted or at least made progress on 16 of the 20 points. That was always something we cited for years as an example of the impact we could have."

Reed continued to meet periodically with Norval. "I never had a short meeting with him. It would be an afternoon, three or four hours. We talked about one issue after another and certain politicians he liked and didn't like. He sort of slouched in his chair in a comfortable way. You would get long pauses sometimes and thoughtful moments. I thought he was the quintessential All-American entrepreneur and decent guy. He was concerned about his business and his country and didn't just want to complain about things, but was always looking for a way to be helpful. He was plain spoken, as honest as the day is long."

Norval took an even greater pro-active stance in the early 1990s. He relayed some deep concerns to his assistants and they wrote up and published a paper with Norval's byline entitled *The American Taxpayer: Why the Burden Is More Than He Can Bear.*

"In reality there is only one group of genuine taxpayers," Norval wrote. "The people who work and produce either a product or a service which is NOT paid for by the government are the only real source of tax dollars this country, state, county, city or township has. Without working people in the private sector, the government wouldn't have a single penny to spend.

"…And those taxpayers are being squeezed dry. The working taxpayer's standard of living has declined dramatically over the past two or three decades. In terms of real buying power, the working taxpayer hasn't had an increase in wages in 30 years. Why? Because the working taxpayer has been forced to carry an ever-increasing share of the burden heaped on him by a bloated, out-of-control government."

This was the core of Norval's message in an eight-page "Urgent Bulletin," dedicated to the employees of Morbark Industries and "thousands of other private companies across the country." Norval stated that a solution was to make the government stop competing with private companies, and that any government service that could be done by a private company should be turned over to the private sector, creating jobs and opportunities for real taxpayers and taking people away from the public trough.

"You might ask why I am publishing these thoughts," Norval wrote. "When you're past 70 years old and you've been in business and employing people for close to 50 years, you've seen a lot. You've been through the depression and World War II and you've seen the creeping paralysis that's gripping this country. I'm not concerned for myself, I'm concerned for the young people, the next generation who live in the greatest country on earth. I'm concerned that it's being destroyed by high ranking politicians of the state and federal governments who appear to be only concerned about the next election." Norval worried that the dream he had experienced was moving out of the reach of America's youth as government continued to choke the free enterprise system, meanwhile amassing more than $3.6 trillion of debt as of 1991.

The strong response to his paper prompted Norval to found Real Taxpayers of America. He established a token dues of $2 per person. At first he solicited members from the immediate area and began publishing and distributing a newsletter. But Norval had a big grassroots vision. "We can organize thousands, even millions, of real taxpayers across the country. For the first time, real taxpayers will speak with a unified voice that cannot be ignored by our political leaders and policy makers."

RTA quickly established broad positions on various issues: privatization of government services; cuts in property tax; reforming the health care system; kicking the unions out of government; overhauling the political system; changing the legal system; stopping government waste and inefficiency; education reform. Each newsletter became more specific on these positions. For example, calling for an education turnaround in Michigan, RTA proposed repealing all school related property taxes and raising an equivalent amount of revenue through sales and income taxes; giving each school age student in Michigan an equal amount of money for education through a voucher system; and merit-based compensation for administrators and teachers.

Following a successful membership drive in the central Michigan counties of Isabella and Mecosta, the campaign extended to the entire 10th Congressional District, running through the center of the lower peninsula from north of Lansing to Traverse City. The short-range goal was to recruit 10,000 members, and then use the 10th district as a blueprint for other districts and states, driving toward a large, nationwide membership. What Norval was putting together was something that resembled the Tea Party two decades before there was a Tea Party.

But only a couple of years into its existence, RTA began to lose momentum. RTA and Norval endorsed Ross Perot and his populist principles for president in the 1992 election. Norval was somewhat skeptical about Perot initially, doubting anyone running as an independent could have much of an impact. But Perot's no-nonsense practicalism won over Norval. "As a successful businessman himself, Mr. Perot realizes that the road to economic growth and prosperity will be paved by entrepreneurs who start and build companies and create jobs," Norval said. "The country is in big trouble because of politicians. Ross Perot is not a politician. He doesn't owe any favors."

Perot received an impressive 19% of the popular vote, while Bill Clinton edged George H. Bush for the White House. While this took some wind out of Norval's sails and that of RTA, a much more serious concern began to weigh on Norval. As his nephew Gary Bardos recalled, "This was when Nub's health was turning."

FIVE

Morbark Industries
Winn, Michigan
October, 1997

Norval Morey is dead at age 77 and now his son, Lon Morey, is in charge of the company Norval founded. One morning a few weeks after the funeral, Lon walks into Norval's office to begin the process of clearing it out and make it his own. Lon and his father were different types of people. Norval had a knack for solving problems born of machinery. Lon had found his niche at Morbark by solving the problems of people.

Lon opens up the desk drawer of his father's massive cypress desk and begins sorting through the contents to see what all has been left in there. He starts tossing things into a cardboard box for storage, then he pauses. He locates a few checks, then several more. All are made out to Nub Morey. Lon recognizes the names of several Morbark employees and other people he knows from Winn and Mount Pleasant. The oldest check is dated 1992 and the most recent is just last week. Maybe a dozen checks, worth thousands of dollars, left to sit, uncashed, in a drawer of Norval Morey's desk.

Norval's close friend and confidante, Larry Burkholder, who has been with Morbark for 35 years, is called in. Burkholder grew up on a farm outside of Winn and practically became a member of the Morey famly. He'd been an invaluable lieutenant under Norval.

Lon motions Burkholder over to the desk and hands him some of the checks. Burkholder takes a look and smiles. "They look like checks to me," Burkholder says.

Lon continues to skim through the checks. His father has yet again amazed him.

Burkholder sits down. "Your dad said he didn't want to embarrass anybody by refusing their check, so he just put them in the drawer and let the person think he forgot to cash it."

"Basically giving all these people this money," Lon says.

"Yeah," Burkholder said. "That was Nub."

"What else am I going to find in here?" Lon asks.

Burkholder shrugs.

"Probably a bunch of IOU's."

Norval Morey and hunting

An avid and skilled hunter since his youth, with both rifle and bow, Norval like many aging hunters backed away from the sport, but in the late '80s his son-in-law Lucky Robison, also the president of Chiparvestor Inc., got Norval back into it. They first hunted on some property Norval had purchased from one of his employees. They had hunted it for a couple of years when Norval asked Lucky to find out who owned the adjoining property and they would buy it. Lucky found out and started the dialogue with the man and made him an offer. The man looked at Lucky and said if it's such a fair offer, you sell me your land for that amount per acre. Lucky went back to Norval with this latest development and Norval sold the man his property.

Lucky and Norval then started hunting on 130 acres Norval owned that he later

Norval's daughter, Betty, was of great assistance to Norval as his health declined.

sold through the years to Lucky and Lucky's wife Betty, Norval's daughter. Lucky would drive Norval to Norval's blind, have lunch with him and walk back to his own blind. "Nub always had something good to eat and I like to eat, so it worked out rather well," Lucky recalled.

Norval planned out 12 deer blinds and had a carpenter build them. Lucky asked Norval what he was going to do with all of them, and Norval replied he was going to sell them. "To my knowledge the only one that was ever sold was one he donated to a fundraiser for a young man running for judge," Lucky said. "The rest of them he gave away. Now today there are people making and selling blinds all over Michigan. Just ahead of the times again."

Norval was showing some early health issues one deer season and wasn't sure if he was going to hunt. Lucky told Norval he would drive Norval to his deer blind and that if Norval got a deer, for Norval to drive over to Lucky's blind and Lucky would help Norval take care of the buck. The first day of the season Lucky thought he heard a shot over Norval's way, but Norval never came over. Around noon Lucky walked to Norval's blind but Norval was gone. Later Lucky found out that Norval had indeed shot a buck but didn't want to bother Lucky so he drove his Cadillac over to the buck and tied a rope around the deer's neck and started off down the road.

"Now this is a black top road mind you, so Nub stayed off to the side and got about half way home when a man stopped him thinking the deer had fallen off Nub's car," Lucky recalled. "Nub said no, I just could not lift him." The man helped Norval load up the buck and when Norval got home he drove the car around his house and to the basement garage where he had a small hoist. He not only got the deer out of the car, but gutted him and skinned him. Norval decided to can the deer so Lucky and Betty went down to assist in this process. Norval's wife, Jeri, wasn't at all pleased with the idea of cooking and canning the deer in her house, but they proceeded with it and were about half done when all of a sudden there was a loud bang.

"When we went to the kitchen to see what had taken place, there was glass and venison all over the kitchen," Lucky said. "After checking it out we came to the conclusion that Nub either did not add enough water to the pressure cooker or no water! Either way the results were a mess." Betty took on the task of cleaning it up, while Norval and Lucky finished preparing the remainder of the deer.

Michelle White, Norval's step-daughter, recalled when Norval invited her husband Ed to go hunting with him. When Norval came to pick him up early in morning, Ed was all layered up against the cold. Norval looked at Ed's outfit and chuckled. He then explained to Ed he would not be needing all those clothes. When they arrived at the deer blind, Ed realized why. "The place was heated and carpeted, with big lounge chairs and magazines on the table," Michelle said. "It was a real nice place."

Norval Morey and food

Norval's knack for growing vegetables was an asset to his neighbors at Lake Isabella. In the summer, after running the show at Morbark all day, he would come home, harvest and then share peas, corn, beans and tomatoes with anyone who wanted them. He hinted at times that he had a secret formula for making things grow, but Michelle couldn't recall exactly what it was. Decomposed wood mulch was her guess.

"I don't know how all these talents could come in one package," Michelle said. "He had so many tools in his basket."

One of these tools was Norval's ability to put a meal on the table.

"He just had a natural ability to cook," said his daughter Betty Robison. "He didn't use recipes." He cooked the Thanksgiving meal, baked his own bread based on his mother's way and made delicious cakes.

Norval Morey and forestry equipment

The patents kept coming. Before he was done, Norval had been issued close to 20 patents on a vast range of wood processing equipment. A patent for a circular saw blade for feller-buncher sawheads, issued to him in 1993, was one of his last. The last patent he filed for, in 1995 when he was 75, was for a hoziontal wood waste grinding machine. Morbark would eventually call it the Wood Hog and it could operate with a grinding drum or a hammermill. Norval didn't appear to be slowing down much, and neither did Morbark, as the size of the factory increased to 1.6 million square feet.

Indeed Norval mastered many tasks and hobbies. He built a great business from scratch. He accumulated tremendous wealth. He hobnobbed with the most powerful man in the world. But about this same

Illness didn't keep Norval from making the rounds.

period in the early 1990s, Norval ran into something that, as hard as he tried, he couldn't overcome: His health. The illness that would eventually take his life came on gradually, and slowly but steadily ate away at his very active life.

There had been health issues before. For a period some years earlier Norval would nearly pass out at any given time. There was difficulty in properly diagnosing it, before Norval was determined to be hypoglycemic, which is low sugar in the blood. It didn't have to be treated, but Norval needed to be aware of it because when he went without food for very long

he would have symptoms. He also had some congestive heart failure and aortic stenosis. The aorta is the main artery carrying blood out of the heart. When blood leaves the heart, it flows through the aortic valve into the aorta. In aortic stenosis, the aortic valve does not open fully, decreasing blood flow from the heart. Norval's mother, Hazel, suffered from congestive heart failure. Norval worried about it, but again it wasn't something that seriously impaired him physically, at least until later when it integrated with other health problems.

In 1992, he happened upon the disease that would lead to his death during a routine blood test. His local physician told him the test revealed too many red blood cells, or in physician's terms, the hematocrit was too high. The treatment was too take out a little blood, called a phlebotomy. Minus two pints of blood, Norval received word that he was okay now.

But Norval wasn't okay. He started feeling painfully stuffed after eating, was having night sweats and began losing weight. He could feel an enlargement in the left upper part of his abdomen, and a little research indicated it was possibly his spleen. He went back to the local doctor, who sent him to Mayo Clinic in Rochester, Minnesota. Nub had been going to Mayo for years to get his regular physical. He went over this time and hooked up with a hematologist, who took one look at the blood cell count and did a bone marrow biopsy. The doctor discovered that Norval's bone marrow was scarring and wasn't manufacturing blood cells like it was supposed to do. Because the bone marrow wasn't functioning properly, the spleen was attempting to produce blood cells, but these were immature red blood cells that were becoming trapped in the spleen. As a result, the spleen was becoming enlarged. Norval's condition was called Agnogenic Myeloid Metaplasia. In some cases the liver as well attempts to produce blood cells to make up for the bone marrow deficiency.

At the time, it was one of those blood disorders that wasn't well understood. The prescribed treatment was to radiate the spleen and shrink it. Norval traveled once a year to Mayo for the radiation, which helped for a while, but then the same painful symptoms returned. Norval's spleen would enlarge to the size of a football. His visits to Mayo increased for the radiation treatment, as his spleen would enlarge again after only three months. Norval had generally kept his condition and these trips to Mayo to himself, but now he reached out to Craig Price. "I'm in trouble," Norval told Price. "This is what they're telling me." In early 1995, the physicians told Norval they couldn't continue to administer the treatment. It had become ineffective and potentially dangerous to other parts of his body.

Craig Price, from Mount Pleasant, had started employment at Morbark in 1989 as the health and safety director. Morbark had put an ad in the newspaper seeking a paramedic. Price knew why. A few months earlier, Price went on an ambulance run out to the Morbark plant after a worker sustained serious injury. That injury prompted Morbark to look for a skilled paramedic. When Price arrived for the interview, Norval invited him into his office. Norval said right away, "I don't know if this is the right thing to do, but I want my people to be safe and with better first aid, but what I really want is a safety department."

After two hours of conversation, Norval hired Price. After six weeks of learning the ropes around the plant, Price was called into Norval's office and learned of his first real project. Morbark had been cited by the Environmental Protection Agency for leakings from underground tanks. "How should we handle it?" Norval asked. Price did some fast research and recommended to Norval that they pull the tanks out of the ground and put everything above ground. "I learned really fast what you tell Mr. Morey," Price recalled. "The next day he had Gary Bardos out there digging the tanks out. I had to scramble because I had to notify people what we were doing." Everything was cleaned up and Morbark received a clean bill of health in just a few weeks.

Right after that, Norval pulled in Price again and told him he was now in charge of the security department and the custodial department as well. Suddenly Price had a dozen employees under him. "I got to work from really the bottom up," Price said. "I started working with the solid waste. I loved every minute of it." Norval kept expanding Price's job description. Price changed the paint process in the factory. He continued to improve hazardous waste disposal.

But by now Price's job description included another task: that of Norval's caregiver. Norval's regressing health really hit home to Price when Norval returned from a trip to Mayo in 1995. Norval had caught a severe cold and his congestive failure was acting up, making it difficult to breathe. This prompted Price to escort Norval to a hospital in Alma. Price recalled, "They loaded him with lasix trying to get this fluid off because his feet were swollen. That was the wrong thing to do, and by the next morning he was unconscious and in ICU. His kidneys actually shut down, too." They brought Norval around the next morning and a day later Price and Norval's son, Lon, and daughter, Betty, had convinced Norval to go to see his cardiologist at Mayo, which sent their plane over to pick them up. Once there, Price recalled, "We finally convinced them to give him some fluid, rather than take fluid off, and within an hour he was awake, sitting up, coughing and coming out of it."

For several months the discussion was about whether to do surgery to repair the bad valves in Norval's heart, but in the end the surgeons didn't think Norval would get enough benefit to warrant surgery. His heart wasn't quite bad enough.

"We made many trips over there trying to keep him tuned up the best we could," Price recalled. "Then right in there he had them take his spleen out. That was kind of the beginning of the end."

What was frustrating, Price said, was that the Mayo physicians never really explained thoroughly the ramifications of removing the spleen; that is, what was going to happen with all these immature cells and what part of the body was going to make cells?

They removed Norval's spleen in early December 1996. Bleeding complications kept him in the hospital longer than anybody had expected. Price recalled that the only time Norval became depressed was for a month or so shortly after the surgery. Betty would stay at the Morey home during the night and Price would show up in the morning and remain all day. "We weren't really doing anything for him. He was just scared," Price said. "It's hard to use that word talking about Norval. He didn't give up by any means. He was still as active as he could be. He still did all of the cooking. But he was depressed. That's not unusual to have some depression after major surgery like that."

His daughter Betty, who stayed many nights at her father's home, said Norval would sit by the fireplace at one end of the living room. "He was down there thinking. He didn't like for me to turn on the television. It was very quiet. He didn't want visitors. I had to screen them out."

After several weeks of not leaving the house, Norval said to Price let's go for a ride. They drove around the lake and the neighborhood and returned to the house and did this routine several days. Then one morning Norval said let's go to the shop and Price drove him to Morbark for a short visit and they repeated this a couple of days. Then one morning Norval drove himself to the plant. He had come out of his depression.

But his liver had almost doubled in size as it tried to manufacture the blood cells that the bone marrow could not produce and that the spleen had been incapable of producing. As a result, the liver pushed up on his diaphragm and right lung. Norval's breathing severely worsened, to the point that he had to have ready access to oxygen. They installed liquid oxygen tanks at Norval's home. They put one on his golf cart at home with fifty feet of hose so he could continue to hoe in the garden with his oxygen on. They bolted one in the back of his car and ran the hose up to his seat so that he could use it as he drove back and forth to work. They put another one on his golf cart at the plant, which enabled him to continue to ride through the factory twice a day, stopping here and there to converse with his beloved employees.

It wasn't all sadness. Larry Burkholder relayed a story about a visit Norval made to an automobile dealership while on oxygen. According to Burkholder, Norval got tired of driving his Lincoln and wanted to trade it for a Cadillac. He pulled in to a dealership and laid on the horn, not wanting to get out of the car. When a salesman approached Norval, he saw the oxygen tanks and took off running. He thought they were bombs. Norval drove away cursing.

The complications mounted. Price accompanied Norval to Mayo Clinic several times, either on a plane provided by the clinic or a private jet Norval used out of Hansen Flying Service in Alma. They continued to struggle to keep Norval's blood cell counts high enough. A couple of blood transfusions had only provided temporary relief. He started having kidney issues and needed more diuretics to keep the fluid off, but they weren't working. His breathing worsened.

Price and Betty were with Norval on his last visit to Mayo Clinic. They met with several specialists. "We had cardiology there, hematology, surgery, kidney specialist and we asked what's the next step," Price recalled. "None of them had anything to offer. They said we can't change this situation. They said they could put Norval on medications to help with the cardiac issues in order to get the kidneys to function a little better, but once that was started Norval might never leave the hospital. And once they did that it's going to cause this and this. They just said this is failing, this is failing, this is why it's doing it. They didn't paint a very rosy picture." Price said they also told Norval that he could develop a bleed, and literally bleed to death, or sustain a massive stroke. Norval said he would do whatever was best, get on the medications or not, "but you could tell he didn't want to be in a situation he couldn't get out of."

Betty called the family and updated them on the darkening situation. Her brother, Lon, and her sister, Connie, and Norval's wife, Jeri, and daughters Michelle and Julie immediately flew up. Their arrival agitated Norval who hated all of the fuss being made over him. Michelle had a moment alone with Norval. He made a chilling statement. "They tell me I only have a little time to live. And if I'm not going to get better, I might as well die." Michelle told him he only needed faith as big as a mustard seed. "That's not all that big," Norval replied.

Norval grew increasingly anxious to leave, grabbed Price by the arm and said, "Call me a cab, I'm leaving." The group flew home, and when Norval got out of the car next to his house at Lake Isabella that evening, he coughed up a little blood, then said to Price that his biggest concern was that he would have a massive stroke and he didn't want to linger on in that kind of shape. Norval had talked before to Price of the thought of being helpless and unable to care for himself, and hinted at the alternative. "He was almost saying things like help me out if I get in that situation," Price recalled. "We talked around that topic enough to where I started feeling uncomfortable with it. I had strong feelings for Nub, but I don't know if I could have helped him with that."

Price remained at the house a little while that evening before leaving, and Betty stayed the night. Before Lon left, Norval asked him to have Larry Noch and Debra Lehmann, the company comptroller, to come out in the morning. Noch was head of finance at Morbark and at Norval's request a trustee of Norval's estate. Norval wanted to shift some assets. The next morning at Norval's home Lon met Noch, Lehmann and secretary Suzanne Noble who could notarize any changes. After conducting some business, Noch said he needed to go back to the office to complete the paperwork and come back out. "Get er done," Norval said.

When Noch and his group departed, Lon sat down next to his sick father. Lon and his father had never been able to work closely together, giving it several attempts, and while Lon at times regretted not having a more personal relationship with his father, he also understood the weight his father carried on his shoulders not only at Morbark but as an important provider to the community. Lon began making a serious contribution to Morbark when Norval had put him in charge of the parts department, turning it into a profitable venture. Norval left Lon alone to run it and Lon would hear through the grapevine that his dad was happy with his work. Lon had migrated into personnel, payroll and benefits around 1990, eventually taking it on full time while turning over parts to his cousin Jim Bardos.

Despite their differences, now Lon was on the verge of assuming the leadership of Morbark Industries. He knew he wasn't the visionary his father had been. He knew he never could have built the company and taken it to the level his father did. Through the years Lon had come to appreciate and admire the work Norval had done during his life.

"There's no man I respected more than him," Lon would say, "and no man who could piss me off more than him."

Lon felt he would bring his own attributes to his new role, and perhaps take the company further than his father could have in the dawning 21st century. Two years earlier his father had told Lon that he felt he was holding the company back. He could not let go of control of the company and the company was too big for one person to run in the authoritative manner Norval had always run it. Norval had looked at backing away from day-to-day activities in the late 1980s and brought in Jay Halloran from Michigan Knife as president. But it was short-lived. Halloran and Lon had doubted at the time that Norval could step down.

Had not Norval's health problems compounded, perhaps nothing would be changing now. But the writing was on the wall. Norval and Lon made some small talk, but they sat mostly in silence. Then Norval looked at his son and said, "You're going to have a lot of decisions to make. Listen to your people. They'll guide you right." Norval lowered his head. He had a way about him that when he was done talking you knew it. Lon knew it. After several silent minutes, Lon left the room, went out and talked briefly to Jeri Morey and drove to Morbark. Jeri was headed out to get her hair done. Betty had left for a change of clothes.

Noch and Lehmann returned to the house to finish the changes to Norval's estate. Craig Price also walked in that morning. He could tell everyone was in the middle of conducting some business.

Norval stood up and said to Price: "I'm not going to need you to stay today. I'm not taking any more medication. I want to thank you for helping me." They shook hands and Price departed.

As Price drove back to Morbark, he knew in his heart that Norval probably wasn't going to live out the day.

Noch suggested that Norval should call any family members affected by the major changes and Norval responded, "I'll take care of it." Noch on his way out spoke to Norval's step-daughter Michelle.

Norval was now left at home with Michelle and two longtime family maids, Karen and her daughter Tammy, who were cleaning in another part of the house. Norval walked over to the kitchen and asked Michelle if she knew how to peel a mango. She prepared it and Nub sat at the table and ate the mango and then said he was going to his bedroom to shave and lay down for a while. Michelle followed him to help him get settled. Apparently Norval asked her to put a blanket on the floor in case he became sick to his stomach. Michelle came back outside the room and shut the door, but stayed near it, listening out in case Norval needed anything.

She heard a clanking sound, like something heavy hitting against a table. Then she heard Norval grunt and heard a dull thud. Michelle became scared, frozen. Then she heard the gunshot.

Karen and Tammy came running. Karen asked the stunned

Michelle if she wanted her to take a look inside the room and Michelle said yes. She was too afraid to go in herself. Karen opened the door. The clanking sound had been Norval retrieving a 9 mm pistol. Norval's groan and soft thudding noise occurred when he had rolled over and plopped down on the blanket on the floor with his head on a pillow he had put down. He hadn't wanted to leave a big mess to clean up.

Norval "Nub" Morey died on Thursday, October 30, 1997 at age 77 after an exhaustive several-year struggle to stay alive.

Michelle called the police and Lon and the beauty parlor where Jeri was.

In his office, Lon's first reaction was why hadn't he seen this coming. He recalled now a couple of comments his dad had made in recent years about not wanting to live out his life incapable of caring for himself. "He did it his way," Lon thought.

Larry Noch had only been in his Morbark office for several minutes when Lon called him into his office. "Dad's dead. He just shot himself," Lon said.

Noch returned to his office in shock and sat down. Chills came over him for several minutes. He had just been with the man. He didn't suspect Norval was about to do this, but Noch had been so focused on the estate matters at hand that he wasn't looking for such signs. The chills subsided. Noch assumed Norval had received some terminal news on his health. "In the end there wasn't anybody who was going to tell him when he was going to go," Noch reflected. "He was going to go when he wanted to go." A warm smile came over Noch's face as he sat at his desk. "Norval did what he wanted to do. He did it his way."

Craig Price also received word of Norval's death from Lon in Lon's office, and then Price drove back to Norval's lake house. He took care of it himself, Price thought. Of course he did.

Larry Burkholder was in the lunch room at Morbark when Lon called him with the news of Norval's death. "I knew he was close to being gone the last time I had seen him," Burkholder recalled. When Burkholder found out the cause of death, he recalled a conversation with Norval about how some terminally ill people chose to end their lives. "Like Kevorkian," Burkholder said, referring to the physician who aided the deaths of many of his patients. Norval kind of shrugged. "You've got a gun don't you?"

Norval's communications director Dan Brandon recalled, "I knew he wasn't the type of person who was going to lay in the hospital bed with tubes sticking out of him for two weeks in the process of dying. He didn't like the sound of that and he was the kind of man who took it into his own hands and that's how he did everything."

"Dad wanted to take care of everybody else, but he didn't want anyone having to take care of him," Michelle said. She considered this to have been Norval's biggest weakness.

Larry Reed, the president of the Mackinac Center, reflected that Norval was the kind of man who wanted to be in charge of every aspect of his life. "He got to the point where he felt he couldn't be and that was it."

Lon Morey's first task as the new leader of Morbark Industries was to personally break the news to many of Norval's closest confidantes. His second task, that same day, was to inform the Morbark work force that Norval had died. He assured them that the business of Morbark would continue to live.

Larry Noch recalled the moment: "Lon handled it very well. He got in front of all of those people and talked to them face to face about what it meant to the company and who was going to run things and how it was going to be. He never had to step up to that level while Norval was in charge. He really shined."

The local *Mount Pleasant Morning Sun* newspaper didn't have a Saturday edition, so with Norval dying on a Thursday, Lon hustled to make sure an article appeared in the Friday paper. He called the owner of the paper, who informed Lon they were going to do a front page story. Dan Brandon met Lon at the funeral home and they went to the newspaper office. The owner introduced them to a reporter, and Lon said he had asked Brandon to write the article. But the reporter said he had everything he needed in his file, and never even asked Lon a single question. Lon walked out livid.

The article came out on the front page as promised, but not only reported that Norval had committed suicide by shooting himself, but stated that family members apparently knew of Norval's intentions to do so and didn't do anything about it. The article also mentioned Norval's earlier lawsuit against his nephew, Mike, for patent infringement. Everyone in the Norval camp became furious. There was no reason to bring all this negativity into an article about a man who had done so much for the area. Lon recalled that the backlash was so great that the paper printed a retraction obituary, written this time by Michelle's husband, Ed White, who was a newspaperman himself. Several people wrote letters to the paper on Norval's behalf, though the paper only printed the one from Debra Lehmann from Morbark who was also chairman of the board of The Morey Charter School.

For a long time Lon forbid anybody at Morbark to talk to anybody at the paper. Then he swallowed his pride, asked the editor to come out to the plant, took him around and said there's a heck of story to write here about a man who built a very successful company in this community, and he dies and leaves it to his son and the company continues to thrive. The editor wrote the article and it helped somewhat to lessen the ill-will that the employees and families of Morbark had held for the paper.

On Saturday, November 1, a closed casket memorial service for family and close friends was held on a rainy day at the Lake Isabella home. People sat in chairs assembled near the casket. Craig Price found a seat next to Mike Morey. Larry Burkholder spoke as did some others. Michelle said the Lord's Prayer. Then the popular Frank Sinatra song, *My Way,* came on the stereo to accompany a slide show of photos from different moments in Norval's Morey's life.

Price recalled: "It was extremely difficult to keep your composure in that room, but when 'I Did It My Way' came on, it was (impossible)."

"It was such an appropriate song," Lon recalled. "Dad loved that song too, because I think he believed it."

Betty stayed away. She couldn't go back into the house where he had died. The pain of losing him was so acute. One of her consoling thoughts during this period was that her dad and her uncle, Harry, had made amends before their deaths. Norval's younger brother, Harry, who always kept the party lively and who could get under Norval's skin in a heartbeat, had taken ill with cancer and died January 21, 1996 at his home in Winn at age 67. Norval and Harry hadn't talked for several years and at various gatherings purposefully avoided each other. No one could quite pinpoint the reason why, unless Harry felt his contributions to Morbark through the years had not been fully appreciated; or it could have simply been a typical brothers' spat that refused to dim. Then not long before Harry's passing, Betty accompanied Norval to Harry and Wilma's farmhouse in Winn. "Harry and dad talked for hours," Betty recalled. "We were thrilled they were talking."

With Norval's passing, following the deaths of Milford, Burnell, Mildred (who had died in 1985 of brain cancer) and Harry, the original eight siblings of Loyal and Hazel Morey had declined to three—Lucille, Leo and Ralph.

On Saturday, November 8, another service for Nub, this one open to the public, was held in the gymnasium at the newly completed Morey Charter School. Dan Brandon did a rush job to write, round up numerous photos and print an impressive 24-page memorial magazine on Norval that was handed out to the visitors. It included a condolence letter from Michigan Governor John Engler. "Norval's death marks the passing of a legend," Engler wrote. "He never forgot his roots. He quietly helped countless people overcome their 'bad luck.' He gave back and he gave back." The place was packed with Morbark employees, associates, vendors, area residents and long-time family friends, all of them very much aware of how much Norval had given back.

Mackinac Center President Larry Reed delivered a eulogy that people still remember. "I always felt stronger by simply being in his presence," Reed said during his talk.

Reed continued: "Those who didn't have the pleasure of knowing him well, but might have met him briefly, probably came away thinking this guy Norval Morey was a little different, but in a positive, attractive sort of way. He was like the round peg that doesn't quite fit neatly into the square hole. He could be cantankerous, but that was because he didn't suffer fools gladly. He could be impatient, but that was because he wanted to get things done. He didn't exactly speak the King's English, but that never mattered because he always made eminently good sense. He never cared much for kings anyway."

Norval's old friend and Morey family friend Ron Demlow also said a few words that day. Demlow had run into Norval at a luncheon shortly before Norval's death. He reminded Norval of the evening back in the mid-60s when the two of them had attended a fundraiser in Grand Rapids and seen three future presidents at once—Nixon, Ford and Reagan.

"Oh, man!" Norval said, perking up. "I had forgotten that. What a dinner that was!"

Norval was buried in nearby Union Cemetery, where he had purchased burial plots for so many others of his family.

"Some people wouldn't believe it if I told them Norval is in heaven, but I'm positive he is," said his sister Lucille. "I believe that some day I will be reunited with my sister and all my brothers there."

On an early spring morning in March of 1997, the president of the Mackinac Center for Public Policy, Larry Reed, and the Center's development officer, Jim Kostrava, pulled into the parking lot of Morbark Industries in the small town of Winn, Michigan. They came to a stop in a parking spot marked for visitors, but neither man got out of the car. Instead they chose to go over once again the strategy they'd dis-

Norval stands outside the blacksmith's shop where he worked on the first portable debarker, which he later salvaged.

cussed on their way over from Midland. Reed was somewhat anxious about his mission on this day, which was to ask Morbark's feisty, innovative, conservative founder, Norval "Nub" Morey, for one million dollars.

Reed was approaching 10 years as president of the Mackinac Center, a state-based group that promoted free enterprise and individual rights over government regulation. The Center already had a few solid success stories under its belt, such as swaying the 1990 Michigan gubernatorial race with the small book called *Michigan: An Agenda of the 90's*. Norval had given the Center a $50,000 grant to pay for printing 50,000 copies of the book and distributing them statewide.

Now Reed was ready to take the Mackinac Center to the next level. Changing times and expanding agendas called for big money donations. Reed's development officer stressed to him there should be no more going in and talking to wealthy people and being content to ask for a $5,000 donation. "We're leaving too much on the table," Kostrava said.

They had speculated over whom they could approach for the Center's first million dollar gift. Norval Morey, the greatest entrepreneur they had ever known, quickly came to mind. Reed had a personal relationship with Norval, dating back to when Norval supported Reed as the Center's first president, and even before that when Norval backed Reed in an unsuccessful run for congress. Norval, they figured, understood and epitomized what the Mackinac Center was all about as well as anybody, and he was a man of means.

Now as Reed and Kostrava sat in the car they rehearsed this tricky mission. Since Reed knew Norval better, Reed would pose the million dollar question. "And if Norval resists at first, don't take it back," Kostrava said. "Don't be too quick to say we'll accept something smaller. Make the case, be persistent and only back off if you think you pushed too far." Reed prepared himself mentally to face the tough questions that would surely come his way. The last thing Reed wanted to do was to make Norval angry. Norval had been good for donations in the past and in all likelihood would keep supporting them in the future as long as they kept him happy.

Reed and Kostrava straightened their ties and walked into the Morbark office building.

The first half hour of the meeting was taken up with the usual ice breakers and small talk. Then Reed got down to business as he and Kostrava sat in front of Norval's desk. Reed started with a few preliminaries, reminding Norval of how far the Mackinac Center had come and how important Norval had been to its development. Norval slouched comfortably in his chair behind the big desk and tugged on his nose with his thumb and forefingers as he listened.

Reed reminded him of the many promises that Reed and the Center had made to keep the people of Michigan informed about their individual liberties and said the impact of the Mackinac Center was just beginning to be felt around the country.

"There is so much more to be done and so much potential out there," Reed said. "There are many people who will step up to the plate and do a major gift to the Center, a multi-year gift, if they saw somebody take the leadership role in that."

Reed went on for several minutes and cut to the chase. "Norval, you are a very special person to us. You're what we call a true believer."

Reed explained what he meant; that some people supported the Center because they liked where the Center stood on one issue or another, perhaps because it affected their bottom line. They weren't necessarily thinking long-term.

"But you're a man who understands the core philosophy," Reed said. "You understand the principles of liberty and limited government that animate all of our work, and you're in this not because if we succeed it helps Morbark's bottom line, you're in it because you know we can help make a freer society for your kids and grandkids. You're thinking long term. You're a true believer."

Then Reed struck: "So I want to make an ask of you that I don't think at this point I can ask of anybody else. Nub, we would like you to become our first one million dollar giver."

Norval had no reaction at first. He appeared to be rewinding Reed's presentation and request in his brain. His response, when it eventually came, was terse and a letdown to Reed.

"What? You want a *million* dollars?"

Reed was certain he'd made Morey mad, the one thing he had not wanted to do. Reed now looked over at Kostrava, who was sitting there quiet as a mouse. The two of them exchanged a quick, nervous glance. Reed could have taken the request back at that point, watered it down some, but he remembered what Kostrava had said. Reed pushed ahead.

"That's right," Reed continued. "If we can't ask it of you, who else can we ask it of? Just think what we can do with that money, think of the additional potential we can draw in support to the Center if you step forward and become our first. What a message that would send! We could start new programs to educate young people instead of waiting for them to become legislators and then working on them, which is like locking the barn door after the horse has left."

Norval still hesitated. "Well, you know you come over every year and I always give you something," Norval said. "I give you $50,000 for that book and now you want a million?"

"Yes," Reed said.

"Well, what would you do with a million?"

Reed could tell Norval was softening. Reed provided more specifics. An hour later, he was still talking, and then there was a pause.

"Well," Norval said. "I think I can do three million."

Reed glanced at Kostrava, who was wide-eyed, and then back at Norval. Reed wasn't sure he had heard correctly.

"What did you say? Did you say three million?"

Norval nodded.

Years later Reed would be a little hazy on what anybody specifically said after that. They all shook hands and Reed and Kostrava left the office. They had been in Norval's office nearly four hours. Driving back to the office, Kostrava was full of praise and slaps on the back for Reed. "You didn't take it back!" Kostrava said.

Reed recalled, "I never knew Norval to say one thing and do another, so I left the meeting knowing he was going to do it."

Norval, always good with numbers, was already figuring out how he was going to do it even as they conversed. In much the same way he had gifted term interest bearing notes to his employees and family members, he would deposit $1 million in a promissory note at the bank in Mount Pleasant and attach terms to it. Every quarter there would be an interest payment at one percent below prime paid by the bank to Mackinac Center for the first 10 years, and then for the second 10 years the million dollar principal itself in addition to the interest each month would be paid out, 10% a year, so that over a 20-year period all of it would be paid out.

The gift would come from The Morey Foundation, which Norval had founded in 1990. On March 10, 1997, Norval wrote the following letter to Reed:

Dear Larry:

It is my pleasure to write this letter confirming my personal commitment to support the Mackinac Center in the amount of $1,000,000. I am confident you will see that these funds are put to good use.

I am able to assist this cause financially today because when I started my company, markets were truly free and business was virtually unregulated. This freedom opened the door to opportunity, success, expansion and hundreds of good paying jobs. I understand what the free enterprise system allowed me to do and I want to help preserve that system.

The Mackinac Center is a strong voice for free enterprise. You and your staff have done an excellent job of presenting carefully researched arguments in favor of individual freedom and responsibility, market-driven economics and smaller government. The citizens of Michigan are fortunate to have The Mackinac Center in the state, and, as founder of The Morey Foundation, I am pleased to be able to lend my support to the cause.

Best of luck in your work. I trust you will keep us informed of your progress.

Sincerely,

Norval K. Morey

Norval's gift would go toward general operations of the Center. Two months later, the Mackinac Center purchased the abandoned Woolworth's building in downtown Midland and embarked on a $2.5

million capital campaign to reconstruct it into the Center's new head-quarters. While Norval's donation was separate from the building campaign, it served to lift the Mackinac Center to new heights. The building campaign was quickly successful and the construction project progressed just as rapidly.

Reed didn't tell Norval because he wanted to surprise him, but part of that construction included a major conference room and they planned to name it the Norval K. Morey Conference Room. They would invite Norval over for the dedication.

But Norval never knew any of that, since he died the month before the new headquarters opened. Norval's son, Lon, and other family members participated in the dedication. The letter Norval wrote to Reed is framed outside of the Norval K. Morey Conference Room.

Norval Morey was a generous soul whose passing did not put an end to his support of philanthropic, educational and political pursuits. In fact, it served to increase it because in his will, Norval left the majority of his assets to The Morey Foundation, valued at $35-$40 million, under his son Lon's direction.

"He provided for his family, not through his death, but while he was alive, whether *Norval's generosity to the community and region was unknown to many on the outside.*

through gifts to trusts, or allowing them to become shareholders of the companies he created," commented Larry Noch, trustee of Norval's estate. "He felt like he had done all he wanted to do for all those he wanted to do it for, and cleared the way for us to give it all to the foundation and keep the IRS out of his pocketbook. That was one of his primary objectives. He wanted to make sure the IRS didn't get it."

Norval's extensive giving to others is one of the characteristics most overlooked about Norval by those outside of Isabella County. Some call Norval the father of wood energy, but few in the industry he championed realized the extent to which he helped raise up the small village where he was born.

Winn is the little village with the mixed up name, a community that waited hopefully for a railroad spur that never came. What they got instead, some half century later, was one man who impacted the community more than any train could have. And while the sheer number of jobs he brought to Winn by taking Morbark to such a high level might be his greatest legacy, his lifelong habit of lending people a hand is especially noteworthy.

"When he was in the service he'd write and always enclose a few dollars in his letters," said his sister, Lucille Towne. "I was working in Alma doing housework and made only a dollar or two a week and that meant a lot."

Back in the 1960's, after a second marriage had taken her to California and after it failed, Lucille and her four children were left basically stranded on the West Coast without any money. Norval brought them back home. He looked after Lucille's children as they were growing up and he put Lucille through nursing school. Nub also paid to have a house built for his little sister.

Lucille turned 87 in 2012—the last surviving Morey sibling. Norval's brother, Leo, died the year after Norval in 1998. Brother Ralph died in 2010.

"He not only helped his extended family, but plenty of others, too," Lucille said. "People don't even know half the things he did to help out."

Lucky Robison recalled that Norval loved to be around children and supported the 4-H Club auction every year. Norval asked Robison to start going to the auctions with him in the early 1980s. "At these auctions he quite regularly bought the Grand or Reserve animals in each category plus any employees' animals that were there," Robison said.

At an auction in 1984, Norval looked at Robison and said they were going to pick a price point and buy every animal that did not meet the price. The steers were getting ready to sell and Norval asked Robison what the going price was and Robison said for those size steers between 85-90 cents a pound. Norval told Robison to start bidding and to not let any animal go for under $1.00 per pound. "The place went wild as the bidding got going and people figured out what was going on," Robison recalled. "We bought 16 steers that year and the parents were coming up to us and thanking us for our support."

The old story goes that the Methodists were held up in a meeting trying to decide how to spend $100. Norval wasn't a church-going person, quite the contrary, but he was at the meeting and he sat there listening to the arguments. Some of the deacons wanted the money to be put toward new carpeting for the church; others wanted it to be used for a list of maintenance woes at the aging structure. Some suggested putting it toward building a new church. After an hour Norval walked out. He found his his right-hand man and brother-in-law, Thurman Barrett, and told him to build a new church on property Norval owned. The next day they were digging a hole and building a new church.

Norval went to the next church meeting and said, "Now take your damn $100 and spend it on carpet for the new church."

His son Lon said, "When he made up his mind to do something, he was not a patient man."

Many of the worthy causes Norval funded likely will never be made public. "He never expected to be paid back for things," Larry Burkholder said. "Even though he was a professed atheist, he was instrumental in building not one but two churches (the Catholic one, where his brother Burnell was a member, along with the Methodist one). He had a sense of community that went back to his lumber camp days. If somebody was down and out and asked for a hand, he helped them."

The Norval K. Morey Cancer Center in Mount Pleasant was made possible through a donation from The Morey Foundation. The center, opened in 2005, is now a part of the larger McLaren Cancer Institute in

Flint. It provides state-of-the-art external beam radiation therapy, chemotherapy, bone marrow biopsies and blood transfusions to residents of Isabella County. Because of Morey's gift, local cancer care is available. To date, the cancer center has treated some 3,000 patients. In 2010, The Morey Foundation helped organize and fund a 5th Anniversary celebration to which former patients were invited to share their stories and mingle with doctors and other cancer survivors.

Norval barely had a sixth grade education. It was only later in life that he came to value education. This is one reason why in 1996, Norval and his son Lon, through The Morey Foundation, chartered and built the Morey Charter School in Shepherd. The school, which emphasizes basic skills and vocational education, opened its doors in August 1997, just two months before Norval passed away.

Perhaps remembering his own bad experience in grade school, Norval said he wanted teachers at the school to be encouraged to develop new and innovative ways to help students learn. He also wanted to make sure the teachers were knowledgeable in their subjects and compensated based on their abilities and contributions to the school.

Even while on oxygen and in failing health, Norval made regular visits to the school construction site to see how the project was coming along.

A plaque stating 10 key principles of the school, which Morey laid out, hangs in every classroom:

* Each student is provided with the opportunity for a solid, basic education in the core academic subjects.

* The academic school day is devoted to teaching and learning reading, writing, mathematics, science, geography, history, government and economics.

* Instruction is individualized to meet the unique learning needs of each student.

* Technology is integrated into the learning environment of each classroom.

* Career awareness, exploration and vocational training are integral components of the K-12 experience.

 * Students are given many opportunities to learn about and understand how their local, state and federal government function.

 * Structured before-and-after school academic programs are offered each day.

 *Students are required to be honest and respectful of each other and school rules are consistently enforced. Thus preparing students for productive, self-reliant lives in a free society.

 * Families have the opportunity to be active partners in their child's education.

 * Teachers are provided with the assistance, class size, training and tools they require for the achievement of excellence in the classroom.

Today, the school, now called Morey Public School Academy, operates as a pre-kindergarten through 8th grade program with 120 students enrolled. Instruction is organized into an elementary and middle school program that features a Montessori approach.

In addition to his individual giving, Norval encouraged Morbark employees to get involved in a number of community causes, including an annual Red Cross blood drive and United Way campaign. Morbark employees still collect toys every Christmas for the Toys for Tots program. The company donates workers and brush chippers during Winn Clean-Up Days each year and has twice sponsored the 980th Quartermaster Company, an Army reserve unit based in Bay City.

Some years after Norval's death, his nephew Gary Bardos invited Norval's three children, Connie, Betty and Lon, over for dinner. After Norval had died, his wife Jeri had given away some of his things to various family members. Gary ended up with Norval's military jacket from World War II.

"I told my wife this doesn't belong to me," Gary recalled. "I went and got the uniform out and we gave it to Lon. He didn't know it was still around. He went in the back and put it on, and when he came out it was the picture of Nub."

Four years after they buried Norval in the family plot, Jeri Morey died. The week prior to the former secretary's death at age 62 from complications associated with emphysema, Jeri told her daughter Michelle she kept having a dream that she and Nub were dancing.

"I really feel like he was there with her when she was sick and he was waiting for her," Michelle said.

Norval's first wife, Phyllis, and mother to their three children, died on March 25, 2008 at age 84. She lived for many years in the house Norval purchased for her on the river in Mount Pleasant, before she sold it and bought a condo in Mount Pleasant. She died there, with her children Betty and Lon at her side. Her third child, Connie, had died in 2006 at age 60.

Once, when son-in-law Ed White called Norval for advice after he had run over a deer and damaged his car, Norval responded in typical fashion. "Does the car drive?" Norval asked. "Yes," White answered. "Well then drive it!" Norval said.

Getting to the heart of the matter, whatever it might have been, surely was one of Norval's most enduring qualities.

Norval Morey was still receiving patents even after his death. In February 1998 he was issued a U.S. Patent Number 5,713,525 for a "horizontal comminuting machine."

EPILOGUE

Lon Morey stands in the foundation remnants of his dad's first home.

Morbark finance director Larry Noch had always worked closely with Lon Morey on employee benefits such as the 401k, but after Norval's death they spent more time together as Noch brought Lon up to speed on the items Norval and Noch had worked together on, such as litigation and banking arrangements.

Two similarities between Norval and his son began to stand out to Noch. One was that they both said what was on their mind. "They're not concerned about how people might take it, whether it's politically correct or the timing of it is appropriate or not," Noch said. "If they were thinking it, they'd just say it."

Another similarity was their concern about their employees. "They both thought about that first," Noch said. "What does this mean to the employee? How do we keep them employed? That wasn't just lip service."

When Lon took over, he immediately recognized some shortcomings in the company. One of them was employee relations. While his dad was always fair with the employees, he didn't take it far enough, Lon felt. For a while Lon implemented "Lunch with Lon," where his secretary would draw six hourly worker names and invite them to Lon's office for lunch on Monday. Lon also emphasized the hiring and training process. He felt too many employees were being pushed along into roles of responsibility before they were quite ready for it—a situation that would sometimes jump up and bite them down the line.

Lon was also concerned that his supervisors hadn't been allowed to reach their full potential. Norval had admitted as much himself because of the way he controlled the business. Lon took it upon himself to set the direction of the company and allow supervisors to step up and possibly make mistakes, as long as they learned from their mistakes.

Several months after Norval died, Lon started having his managers take Dale Carnegie leadership and training courses. Lon had taken his first Dale Carnegie course when he was 16 and working at Morbark. Also early on Lon began to implement portions of Lean Manufacturing, a program that focused on the elimination of wasted process while enhancing product value for the customer. Craig Price, health and safety director at the time, was a big proponent of it.

An important thing Lon tried not to do was imitate his dad. Whereas his dad made regular rounds through the factory, even when he was on oxygen and riding through on a golf cart, Lon felt he would be undermining his production supervisors and managers by making regular appearances on the line.

Lon also streamlined upper management, reducing the number of board members (who were also VP's). "I don't make a whole lot of decisions by myself," Lon said. "I get the approval of the VP's. They're the ones running the company."

In essence, Lon began to change the culture of Morbark, moving it from a "Norval culture" to a diversely managed operation enhanced by a skilled, results-oriented employee base that was driven to have input and to excel by positive feedback for their work.

"Morbark isn't completely there yet, but we have the starting of a true culture," Lon said.

Another difference between Norval and Lon was there approach to dealer representation. Norval and Morbark were always known for their company stores. The involvement of dealers varied with Norval's mindset at the time.

"Dad never liked dealers," Lon said. "His feeling was why pay somebody twenty percent when we can do it ourselves. I have a different philosophy. Some of our dealers have more staff in selling and service to handle one state than we had to handle the whole world."

It took Lon several years to convince his dealers that Morbark was committed to them, wanted to form partnerships and provide the proper tools to its dealers.

Lon enhanced Demo Days at the Morbark plant, which included live demonstrations of Morbark machinery for dealers and customers. "We have a very impressive plant," Lon said. "If that owner comes out here and sees our facility and meets our people, I can't imagine why they wouldn't want to do business with us."

Almost symbolic of the "fat" that he felt Morbark was carrying, Lon directed the teardown of 400,000 square feet of building. He couldn't get his VP's to agree at first. One wanted to use the space for storage. "That's part of our problem," Lon said to the VP. "We store stuff. We don't need the space."

Another cutback has been in the employee count. Employment had risen to 735 in 2000-2001. Lon himself admitted to neglecting the rapid escalation. It had always been the Morbark way—just keep hiring. An aging workforce whittled down the numbers without layoffs, and then following the recession of 2008-2009, Lon implemented a rotational layoff schedule. Today employment is at about 475.

Then in August 2011, Lon named Jim Shoemaker as president of Morbark, Inc. Shoemaker had joined Morbark in 2003 and was VP of Operations before succeeding Lon as president. Lon retained the title of CEO and Chairman.

The company's product line has continued to expand and diversify since Norval's death, such as the introduction of a shredding machine known as the Predator. In recent years, wood biomass came to be seen as a renewable energy resource, and stirred the development of biomass power plants and wood pellet plants in the United States and overseas. The accompanying need for more chipping and grinding capacity on the ground suited Morbark Industries just fine.

Many "younger" people think wood energy power is a new concept. Norval Morey preached it 40 years ago.

Lon Morey continues to spearhead The Morey Foundation, which continues a pattern of uncommon generosity to the region, a policy set down by Norval from the earliest days of his success. Even as payment of the original $1 million gift Norval made to the Mackinac Center began to wind down, Lon and the foundation gave an additional $1 million to the Mackinac Center in 2005 to establish the Morey Fiscal Policy Initiative. In 2007, The Morey Foundation pledged $1 million to Central Michigan University's College of Education and Human Services for a new education building. The Foundation also contributed $600,000 to the Central Michigan University College of Medicine Scholarship Fund; $1 million to build a local Hospice House; $1.5 million to Children's Discovery Museum; $2.5 million to Central Michigan Community Hospital; $3 million to build Morey Courts, featuring eight basketball courts, three racketball courts and a full fitness center

While not all of the foundation's gifts are as monetarily generous, they're always tremendously effective. For the past eight years the Foundation has sponsored a Talent Contest for all the local high schools of Isabella County. In 2012, the Foundation sponsored the SLIM-to-WIN weight loss contest, which attracted nearly 900 participants, and which paid more than $15,500 to the winners.

Norval's daughter, Betty Morey Robison, lives on Lake Isabella not far from the lakeside home where her father planted his summer flowers and had his garden. Her dad is always in her thoughts. She remembered, while growing up, loving to listen to him, his brother Ralph and sister Lucille talk about the old days. "When he pointed his finger at us, we knew not to interrupt him."

Betty said she and her siblings never knew how much Norval Morey helped people until after his death. "He just never really talked about it."

Fifteen years after his death, Betty will choke up talking about him.

"My father was a big man. He was an inspiring man. He wasn't perfect, but he was perfect to me. I miss him every day."

SOURCES

Norval Morey tapes

Morey family archives

Morbark Industries archives

Timber Harvesting magazine

Pulpwood Production magazine

Rhymes of a Western Logger, Robert Swanson, Harbour Publishing, 1992

Whistle Punks & Widow-Makers, Robert Swanson, Harbour Publishing, 1993

History of the 88th Infantry Division—Blue Devils in Italy, a CD, including commander reports and narratives of the 349th, 350th and 351st regiments, compiled by Gary Smith

Isabella County Times-News

National Personnel Records Center, Military Personnel Records, St. Louis

Infantry Structure, Lt. Col. Hugh Foster http://www.trailblazersww2.org/history_infantrystructure.htm

History of the 745th Tank Battalion History http://www.745tank.com/pages/cover.html

3rd Infantry Division History, The Army Almanac: A Book of Facts Concerning the Army of the United States, U.S. Government Printing Office, 1950.

The bravest of the brave: The 3rd Infantry Division in World War II. Robert Broadwater

Ludington Daily News

We Were There: From Gruber to the Brenner Pass, Compiled by

Headquarters, 88th Infantry Division, Published by Information & Education Section

The Family Tree, Potlatch Forests, Inc. 1938-1939

McCloud Rails: McCloud River Lumber History http://www.trainweb.org/mccloudrails/LumberCompany.html

Weyerhaeuser History http://www.weyerhaeuser.com/Company/CorporateAffairs/History

The McCloud Strike of 1909, James Pruitt

Isabella County Sesquicentennial Commemorative Edition, 2009, The Morning Sun

Clarke Historical Library obituaries link to Chippewa River District Library, Monica Fox, Systems Librarian

Mackinac Center www.mackinac.org

Winn Area Centennial book, 1876-1976, Winn Centennial Committee, Enterprise Printers, 1976

U.S. Census Records, Ancestry.com

Union Cemetery, www.findagrave.com

Other books published by The Donnell Group:
God's Receiver: The Terry Beasley Story
Only Doing My Job: Memories Of A World War II Fighter Pilot
Touchdown Auburn: Memories And Calls With Jim Fyffe
Troy: 1838-2006
Down Through The Years: Great Quotations On Auburn Football
The Church Of The Ascension: A Resurrection Story
St. John's Episcopal Church: A Brief History
Iron Butterfly: A Genealogy
Auburn Man: The Life And Times Of George Petrie
My Times With Coe: Fred Fields And Free Enterprise
Lewis Colbert: The Unlikeliest Auburn Tiger
An Ancient Goddess In Old Mobile
Brother Sid: A Novel of Sidney Lanier